CHICKEN SOUP FOR THE WINE LOVER'S SOUL

CHICKEN SOUP
FOR THE
WINE LOVER'S
SOUL

A Toast to the
Perfect Occasion

Jack Canfield
Mark Victor Hansen
Theresa Peluso

Health Communications, Inc.
Deerfield Beach, Florida

www.hcibooks.com
www.chickensoup.com

We would like to acknowledge the many publishers and individuals who granted us permission to reprint the cited material. Any content not specifically attributed to an author was written by Theresa Peluso. The stories that were penned anonymously, that are in the public domain, or that were written by Jack Canfield, Mark Victor Hansen, or Theresa Peluso are not included in this listing.

Food of the Vine. Reprinted by permission of Dawn Josephson. ©2007 Dawn Josephson.

Muscat Got Your Tongue? Reprinted by permission of Nancy Ann Jackson. ©2006 Nancy Ann Jackson.

What Comes to Those Who Wait? Reprinted by permission of Rod G. Boriack. ©2007 Rod G. Boriack.

A Thanksgiving Toast. Reprinted by permission of Diana M. Amadeo. ©2006 Diana M. Amadeo.

No Good Thing. Reprinted by permission of Elsa Kok Colopy. ©2007 Elsa Kok Colopy.

(Continued on page 215)

Library of Congress Cataloging-in-Publication Data is on file with the Library of Congress.

©2007 John T. Canfield and Hansen and Hansen LLC
ISBN-13: 978-0-7573-0631-0 (trade paper)
ISBN-10: 0-7573-0631-4 (trade paper)

Publisher: Health Communications, Inc.
　　　　　3201 S.W. 15th Street
　　　　　Deerfield Beach, FL 33442-8190

Cover design by Larissa Hise Henoch
Inside book formatting by Theresa Peluso and Lawna Patterson Oldfield

We dedicate this book
to those who cultivate the soil,
tend the vines, and coax the essence
from a humble fruit to create
an enigma that has charmed
man for centuries.

Contents

2. TICKLING THE TASTEBUDS

3. RELAXING RENDEZVOUS

Acknowledgments

Compiling, editing, and publishing a book requires the energy and expertise of many people. First, a huge thank you to our families who support us with love and encouragement. Thank you Inga, Christopher, Travis, Riley, Oran, Kyle, Patty, Elisabeth, Melanie, and Brian.

Behind the scenes there are dozens of talented, enthusiastic staff members, freelancers, and interns who keep the wheels turning smoothly at Chicken Soup for the Soul Enterprises, Self-Esteem Seminars, Mark Victor Hansen and Associates, and our publisher, Health Communications, Inc.

The vision and commitment of our publisher, Peter Vegso, brings Chicken Soup for the Soul to the world.

Patty Aubery and Russ Kalmaski share this journey with love, laughter, and endless creativity.

Patty Hansen has handled the legal and licensing aspects of each book thoroughly and competently, and Laurie Hartman has been a precious guardian of the Chicken Soup brand.

Michelle Adams, Noelle Champagne, D'ette Corona, Lauren Edelstein, Jody Emme, Teresa Esparza, Jesse Ianniello, Tanya Jones, Debbie Lefever, Barbara LoMonaco, Mary McKay, Dee Dee Romanello, Gina Romanello,

Veronica Romero, Brittany Shaw, Shanna Vieyra, Lisa Williams, and Robin Yerian support Jack's and Mark's businesses with skill and love.

We appreciate the work of HCI's editorial department directed by Michelle Matrisciani and the HCI creative team led by Larissa Hise-Henoch whose efforts make each book special. And thank you to the rest of the staff at HCI, who for their sheer numbers must go nameless, who get all of our books into readers' hands, copy after copy, with dedication and professionalism.

Readers around the world enjoy *Chicken Soup for the Soul* in more than thirty-six languages because of the efforts of Claude Choquette and Luc Jutras at Montreal Contacts, The Rights Agency.

Our thanks and appreciation go out to the hundreds of writers who shared their stories about their love of wine. We enjoyed them all and regret that we couldn't publish each one of them.

A special note of thanks to Mandy DeBord for sharing her knowledge of and passion for wine. And thank you to the group of wine lovers who volunteered to help us select these stories; Nora Chesler, Gerald DeShields, Sharon Mason, Monica Ott, Juanita Pacito, Ellen Packo, Sallie Rodman, Teresa Schleifer, Franklin Shenkman, Lisa Trentacosta, Cathy Ward, Dave Wilkins, and Maria Williams.

Introduction

The grape—elegant in its simplicity—through a combination of science and art is turned into wine, which is sensual and complex, mysterious, romantic, and even intellectually stimulating.

Like snowflakes, no two wines are alike. The same variety of grape grown in the same soil can smell, taste, and look different each year—even day to day—yet, fine vintners learn to use what nature gives them; a small yield of grapes one year simply means fewer barrels of high-quality wine.

Winemaking is an art form that began centuries ago. A jar once filled with resinated wine was excavated from the "kitchen" of a Neolithic (8500–4000 BC) home in what is now Iran. Winemaking scenes appear on Egyptian tomb walls dating back to 2700 BC, evidence of a thriving, royal winemaking industry where wines produced in vineyards in the Nile Delta constituted a set of provisions for the afterlife.

Herodotus, the 5th century BC Greek historian, describes shipping wine down the Tigris and Euphrates rivers from Armenia in round, skin-covered boats loaded with date-palm casks to be delivered to Babylon (Iraq). And winemaking in Crete, the largest of the Greek islands, flourished during the roman ages (150 BC–AD 529), when no less than fifteen pottery workshops on the island made clay jars for transporting wine. Remnants of those jars have been unearthed in towns all along the Mediterranean shore. When the Venetians occupied Crete in the early thirteenth century, the local authorities took the first measures to limit vine cultivation to protect a prosperous commodity.

The Catholic Spanish colonists brought winemaking to Mexico in the 1500s, practicing their faith and honoring Christ's sacred act of turning water into wine, but the climate of Mexico proved too harsh. When the Franciscan fathers transported cuttings from Mexico to a more suitable climate in California, winemaking in America began. During the 1800s, Chinese laborers lured to California by the great Gold Rush stayed to work the vineyards that would establish California as one of the premiere vinticultural regions of the world.

In the early twentieth century, immigrants came to the United States dreaming of prosperity. Worldly possessions and treasured momentos, including carefully wrapped grapevines from Italy, Greece, Spain, and France that would be planted in the soil of their adopted home, were packed into satchels and trunks. Vines were tended in small gardens until their roots took hold and the fruit ripened. When the grapes were ready, they would be pressed, and the juice fermented in oak barrels stored in dark, cool cellars dug below homes built with their own hands. When the wine was ready, jugs were filled and carried up to the kitchen where a daily glass, served in a simple tumbler, would accompany each meal. Some of

these new Americans ventured West, and began vineyards in California, Oregon, and Washington that still
exist today.

From those humble beginnings, viticulture has evolved
into a billion-dollar industry of the twenty-first century.
There is a wine for every taste—from the simple to the
sophisticated—and for every pocket—from a few dollars
to several thousand for a bottle.

This beverage has mesmerized poets, artists, philoso-
phers, and leaders of the world; turning some into con-
neusieurs, while others fell into a life of debauchery.

From harvesting the grapes to uncorking a fine bottle,
wine holds a special place in our customs, diet, social life,
and religion. It is as embedded in our culture today as it
was in ancient Egypt.

Wine challenges and engages all of our senses, but smell
most profoundly. We taste only the basics of wine.
Without the aroma, flavors become one-dimensional. Of
all the senses, smell is the one hardest to describe, yet the
one most capable of processing the complexity of wine.

Perhaps that is why describing wine requires a vocabulary dictated by nature. A limitless number of adjectives
are invoked to describe subtle nuances and overpowering
aromas, or to simplify hundreds of variables so that one
can communicate the common structure of a wine.

Our eyes feast on dazzling colors of gold, garnet, or the
shyest pink in a glass. We feel the oily sheen or the silky
sheer of wine, it's lightness or full-body, with our mouth.
And the sound of a cork slipping from a bottle accompanied by the laughter of friends is music to our ears.

Whether it's a jug wine to complement a midday meal, or a fine wine crafted by gifted hands and obsessed over by connoisseurs, enjoying wine is an experience. Wine can turn a mediocre meal into a memorable moment, and the pairings to compliment and enhance one another are endless. The only rule: eat and drink what you enjoy. If that's a full-bodied red with fish, so be it.

Come . . . pour yourself a glass of your favorite red or white, and join our writers in a toast. To the celebration of life, to family traditions, to love and happiness, all made more memorable by the essence of a simple grape.

Salute!

Theresa Peluso

1

DELECTABLE DELIGHTS

Food of the Vine

Good family life is never an accident
but always an achievement
by those who share it.

James H. S. Bossard

"Wine is not drink," my Baba says. "Wine is food."
Baba is the Croatian word for *Grandmother*, and my Baba is the epitome of an Old-World grandmother: a meaty woman with a sturdy, slightly-hunched frame, face creased with deep wrinkles from years of hard work, dressed completely in black (as all good widows are), feet in black sandals revealing worn and dirt-stained toes, and the customary babushka (a headscarf folded and tied under the chin) adorning her head.

Baba, now eighty-two-years old, lived most of her life in what is now called Croatia. When she was growing up, the country was called Yugoslavia. Baba still has a house in Croatia on the island of Pasman (located in the northern most part of the former Yugoslavia), and she goes there yearly to reunite with her only remaining sister and her sister's large family.

Every year she returns from her visit to her homeland with various smuggled items: homemade olive oil, bulbs and bulbs of garlic, fresh bay leaves, prosciutto (a dry-cured ham), and wine . . . lots and lots of homemade red wine.

"Two fingers of wine each day keeps you healthy," Baba always says. As she does so, she holds a juice glass in her right hand and uses the first two fingers of her left hand to illustrate how much wine to put in the glass. Wine glasses are a needless luxury in her eyes, so she always drinks her wine from a juice glass or tumbler.

In the fall of 2005, I accompanied my Baba on her yearly trek to Croatia. After nearly twenty-four hours of traveling, we arrived in Nevidjane, the town on Pasman where my Baba grew up and has her house today. It's a farming island, where cattle and crops are as commonplace as are coffee shops and convenience stores in the States. But unlike farming communities in the States, where a farmer has one large tract of land that also contains his or her dwelling, farmers in Croatia have several small tracts of land situated at various locations on the island.

On several of my Baba's plots she grows red grapes. At each of her grape crops we visited, she picked off one of the plump purple jewels and handed it to me. *"Ovdje. Jesti neki,"* (Here. Eat one.) she would say. Each grape I tasted burst in my mouth with an intensely sweet grape flavor. The grapes were also loaded with tiny crunchy seeds. I spent the majority of the walk between crops picking broken seeds from my teeth.

After our tour of her grapes and a good night's sleep, it was time for the harvest. Baba explained the ways of harvesting very simply: "Locate a mature cluster of grapes.

Hold the cluster away from the vine. Cut it with part of the stem still attached. Place the grape cluster in the basket."

And so I did as instructed, from morning till night. By nightfall, my fingers were worn, blistered, and tired from all the picking and cutting. Just as I was about to drift into a much-needed deep sleep, Baba announced, *"Sutra, mi izraditi vino."* (Tomorrow, we make wine). I couldn't wait.

The next day, fingers still weary from a full day's picking, we headed to the wine press facility. I was expecting to see a large building filled with huge presses and baskets of grapes from all the locals. So when we walked the first of our baskets of grapes to an old and partially caved-in stone house, I was perplexed.

"Baba, what are we doing here?" I asked.

"Stvaranje vino!" (Making wine!) Baba replied.

I followed her through the front door and into the dimly lit space. The entire building was about the size of my living room at home. The opening from the partially caved-in room provided our only light. Baba told me that this used to be her house when she was a girl. It was the house where she and her four siblings were born.

The room smelled of old, fermented wine. The walls were lined with big five-gallon barrels, and in the center was a huge wooden vat. Standing inside the room were six other old women from the town, one of whom was Baba's older sister, Lucia. The other five women were various distant cousins and great-great aunts of mine. With all of them donned in black garb and babushkas, I almost couldn't tell them apart. They stood amongst baskets of grapes and chatted in their native tongue.

"Dobar jutro," (Good morning) I said as I entered the room. The women stopped talking and greeted Baba and me. Lucia broke the pleasantries.

"Brzo. Moramo hitnja," (Quickly. We have to hurry.) Lucia said. Even though Lucia was ninety-five-years old, she had the spunk of a teenager. She pointed to the large vat in the center of the room and said to me, *"Pljusak tvoj grožđe ima."* (Pour your grapes in there.) I did as instructed.

I watched as Lucia removed her sandals, slightly lifted her black skirt, and stepped into a shallow pan of water. Satisfied that her feet were clean, she pulled the bottom of her skirt up to her waist and tucked the hem into her waistband, forming a sort of poofy mini-skirt. She then stepped into the vat of grapes.

Oh my! I thought to myself. *THIS is how they make the wine?!*

Stomp, Stomp, Stomp, Stomp, Stomp, Stomp . . . I couldn't believe my eyes.

I watched Lucia bounce up and down, one foot at a time, as she squished the grapes with her bare feet. Even though her gray hair and wrinkled face confirmed her age, while she was stomping on those grapes, a radiant glow came over her face and she looked twenty years younger. Based on her heavy breathing, I knew it was hard work, but she obviously loved doing it.

After Lucia did her grape stomping time, the next woman in line repeated the process and so the rotation continued. When the sixth woman was completing her grape stomping time, Baba was still making trips back and forth with her baskets of grapes, refilling the vat as the grape level diminished. According to my count, Lucia was next in line for another round of grape stomping, but instead of walking to the vat to do her appointed time, Lucia looked at me, smiled, and said, *"Ti si sljedeći."* (You're next.)

"What? . . . Me? . . . You're kidding, right?"

Lucia laughed as she replied, *"Nijedan. Ja sam ne šaleći se. Ti si sljedeći. Uči."* (No. I'm not kidding. You're next. Get in.)

The other women agreed with Lucia and encouraged me to start stomping. I remained where I stood and just gave an awkward smile. *I am NOT getting in there,* I thought.

Just then one of the women bent down, grabbed my right foot, and started taking off my shoe and sock. The other women joined in and then escorted me to the water pan and up and into the vat of grapes.

Squish. My feet sunk in as if the grapes were quicksand. I had no choice. I started stomping. *Oh yuck!* I thought as I forced a grin on my face. To me, the grapes felt like slime squishing between my toes. Stomp. *Ouch!* Stomp. *Gross!* Stomp. *Ouch!* Stomp. *Gross!*

By the end of my stomping time, my feet were red, scratched, cut, and juice-stained. I had grape seeds, grape pulp, and grape skin packed under my toenails and between my toes. Tiny splinters of grape stems were embedded everywhere in my feet. Even after rinsing my feet in clean water, they still looked stained and dirty, just like Baba's. So *that's* why her feet are permanently this color, I realized.

Even though everyone else present did many more rounds of stomping, I was excused from further duty.

"Njegovateljica stopalo," (Tender feet.) Lucia said as she chuckled.

I agreed: *"Njegovateljica stopalo."*

That evening, back at Baba's house, we opened a bottle of the family's wine from last year's harvest. This one was bottled in an old Coca-Cola bottle. Little bits of grape flesh floated in the red liquid.

🍷 A Simple Fruit

All grapes start out green. Those used for white wines turn various shades of gold or pink, and red varieties turn red, purple, or black. There are over 8,000 varieties of grapes in the world but most are unsuitable for wine making.

After such a hard day's work, everyone drank more than the customary two fingers' worth. And as I tasted this batch of wine, now with the knowledge of all the blood, sweat, and tears that go into making it (literally), I had a new appreciation for the wine itself, as well as the wine-making tradition I was now a part of.

In this Old-World culture, so far removed from the complexities of the modern life I was accustomed to, wine is not only a beverage to be enjoyed; it is also what nourishes the family unit, keeping people and generations together to share an age-old tradition.

Baba was right—wine *is* food: not for the body, but for the soul.

Dawn Josephson

So many wines. So little time.

Wine can be made from an array of grapes or just a single type. The climate of the region affects the taste of the grape, and the ripeness at harvest helps determine the dryness or sweetness of the wine. During vinification (winemaking), the winemaker oversees the picking and crushing of the grapes, as well as the temperature of the fermentation process. Different styles of wine require different fermentation and aging processes. For instance, red wine acquires its color through the grape skins left in with the juice, and storing wine in oak barrels imparts a vanilla and toast aroma.

Red wine is made from black grapes that are fermented with the skin and seeds (the "pips"). The skins stay in contact with the fermenting juice (the "must") which results in the pigment, flavor, and other components that make the wine distinctive. Styles range from light and refreshing, to sweet and fortified, to silky and mellow.

White wine can be made from either white or black grapes, as all but a few grapes yield juice that is colorless. In the making of white wine, the unfermented must does not interact with the skins for any length of time. White wine styles vary from bone dry to golden sweet.

Champagne is produced through a unique process of adding a yeast and sugar solution to dry table wine after which the wine is sealed for secondary fermentation.

Rosé wine is produced from black grapes. The juice is separated from the skins when the desired degree of color is reached and allowed to continue fermenting.

Blush wine originated in California. The skins of the black grapes are left to briefly macerate (soak) with the must and produce a pinkish-blue, coppery-colored wine.

Semi-dry or sweet wines are always either white or rosé, rarely reds. The fermentation is stopped before all the sugar is metabolized by the yeast by warming the wine to room temperature and then super-chilling the must to 40°F for several weeks.

Muscat Got Your Tongue?

*Three grand essentials to happiness
in this life are something to do, something
to love, and something to hope for.*

Jose Addison

S wirl, sniff, sip, and savor. Fine golden threads, known as "legs of the wine," coated the sides of our crystal Riedel goblets. A bouquet of peach, citrus rind, flower blossoms, and papaya filled the air.

On this glorious spring day, my husband and I, still in the courting stage of our relationship, were out enjoying the romantic escape of winery touring along the beautiful wine regions of Oregon. Soft Celtic harp music drifted out of the car as we drove through the pillared gates and made our way up a long, steep hill toward the Willamette Valley Vineyards. A brilliant blue sky devoid of clouds hung overhead while warm rays of sunshine lit the plentiful rows of grapevines, making us feel we'd entered a mini-version of paradise.

Hand in hand we made our way inside the spacious winery, where hosts of people were on hand to talk wine and to pour mouthwatering samples of full-bodied Pinot Noir, oak-barreled Chardonnays, and a delightful tasting

Muscat. There is an art to wine tasting—one my husband and I have learned to appreciate—along with the hard work of the vintners, who for centuries, have created a variety of flavors that speak to the heart, mind, soul, and spirit of faithful wine drinkers.

After tasting a palate-friendly flight of white wines, we each ordered a glass of Frizzanté Semi-Sparkling Muscat and followed the winding staircase up to the tower room. The small rounded room was especially cozy and romantic. Gentle breezes wafted in through the open windows and ruffled my now-husband's dark hair. I imagined the lopsided grin plastered on his face was the same one reflected from mine. We were in love and everything about the moment magnified our feelings.

With a clink of our glasses, we toasted to another day of being together. For almost two years we'd endured the pang of distance, traveling over four thousand miles to be with one another whenever we could. Every precious second that we shared counted. Wine touring had quickly become something we mutually enjoyed, whether along Niagara-on-the-Lake in Ontario, or deep within the Rogue Valley of Oregon.

I tilted the bowl-shaped glass to my lips and let the sweet, golden liquid slide down my throat. The crisp, light-bodied taste tingled in my mouth and quenched my thirst. Half a glass later the wine had loosened both our tongues, and we talked of trips to France, Italy, Spain, and Ireland, and how we longed to reside on property big enough to plant enough vines to make our own wine. Out the windows we gazed at the magnificent view of the valley and all its rolling hills, trees, and rich farmland. Magic was in the air, and the romantic atmosphere intensified our emotions.

I rested my head on his shoulder and listened to his baritone voice as he spoke of dreams, wishes, and goals. Moments later we shared a kiss, and I tasted the musky, fresh grape flavor on his lips. As we parted briefly to catch our breath, tender waves of love washed over me. More than the wine was making me giddy, but it felt right. While I basked in the glow of our kiss, he tripped over words that I knew he'd meant to sound charming, but instead it came out in a garbled mess.

♟ *Tradition*

Mesopotamians were the first people to cultivate grapes and make wine as far back as 8000 BC. Grapes are the fruit of choice for making wine because of their high levels of sugar and their balance of acid and nutrients, which allows for natural fermentation with stable results.

Giggling, I asked, "Muscat got your tongue?" We laughed together, sinking into each other's warmth, and finished our glass of wine. I don't know how long we stayed up in the tower room, but it wasn't nearly long enough.

My husband and I have accumulated many memories of our trips to the Willamette Valley Vineyards, but this day remains closest to my heart. It was the day all lingering doubts of my feelings were erased and I knew I'd found my match. Like a fine vintage wine, our love continues to blossom with age.

Nancy Jackson

What Comes to Those Who Wait?

What is the definition of a good wine?
It should start and end with a smile.

William Sokolin

How long does a divorce last? A few hours squirming in a quiet courtroom? A year of hammering out financial agreements and custody issues? Eleven years of wondering? Eleven years is not what I'd have guessed or chosen to stretch it out to, but that's the way it happened. Try as I might to make the whole process faster, more painless, or a manifestation of great wisdom and discernment, eleven years is just the way it happened.

Nothing helps a decade pass better than a glass of wine in the evening. It gets dark, the neighborhood lights go off one by one, and I grow introspective. To uncork a bottle of something that has traveled a long way between a small green grape hanging on a spindly vine in the sun, to a dark, ruby-red elixir is nothing short of inspiring; amazing. That's precisely what I needed every night of eleven years not knowing where my own journey would take me.

If you love wine, sooner or later you wonder what a really good, expensive bottle of wine tastes like. You know, the kind of wine that has been waiting under a veil of dust in a cool, dark subterranean cellar for years, and is gently slid from the rack at just the right moment in time. The kind of wine that is uncorked and allowed to breathe before a trickle of the dark, red wine is poured into a glass. The kind of wine that smells of warm blackberries, cherries, and fresh-tilled soil.

I couldn't afford a good bottle of wine, but I bought one anyway. I drove to the local wine store and parted with fifty dollars, listening to the assurance of the salesperson that the bottle of Cabernet Sauvignon would age beautifully and come to a rich fullness in time. He promised, "It will not disappoint." It was a gift to myself and an incentive to be patient. There would come a day when I would either celebrate a coming back together with my wife, or mark the painful moving forward of a divorce. On that day, in the quiet of the evening, whenever it would come, I would pull the bottle from the dark shelf in my closet, and mark the time and occasion thoughtfully.

Eleven years passed very slowly. There was a new job, moving to a new state, two young children wondering what was going on, false starts at getting back together, tears, depression, hope, and divorce papers drafted and redrafted. A couple times a year, I would reach into the dark closet and give the bottle a gentle turn wondering when I would open it, and what it would taste like after such patient tending. The bottle probably didn't need turning, but there was something reassuring to me about holding it in my hand and feeling its substance and the coolness of the glass.

Then the day finally came—the one to mark. It was not the joyous occasion of a healing marriage and reunion of the family that I'd hoped for, but it was a final divorce that brought closure and the freedom to live in ways I'd dared not before. I pulled down the long-held bottle of wine to mark the moment in life with friends, Glenn and Chris, who had cared for me without expectation over the years. We gathered for dinner around a meal prepared in a man-ner that I had come to admire Glenn and Chris for; a meal pre-pared with conversation and laughter, full of flavor and spice, offering something familiar and something new. And then there was the bottle of wine. They loved wine, too, and it was a fit-ting pleasure to share this moment with them, the three of us, around a meal.

Glenn pulled the cork, slowly poured three glasses of the very deep red Cabernet, and passed us each a glass. We looked at each other and nodded, toasted

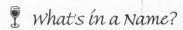

♀ What's in a Name?

A beverage can only be called "champagne" if it is made in the Champagne region of France from Champagne grapes. As early as the 17th century, the English and Spanish learned the fermentation process and added different sugars to white wine to create their own versions of sparkling white wines. Sparkling white wine, similar in texture to champagne, is made in different regions worldwide.

by touching glasses across the table, and sipped knowing that life for me was different from this point on. There was a long, deep sip, and then—oh, my god—could it be any more awful? We puckered and winced and spit the bitter, vinegary wine back into our glasses. Eleven years had not been so kind to the wine I'd coddled and waited for.

We laughed so hard we cried and the humor of the moment perhaps gave my real tears cover. Another bottle of wine was brought out and uncorked. And later, another. There was so much to celebrate even though little was certain, and not much can be promised about life and wine. None of it was what I expected, but I can't say I'd skip the waiting and wondering if I had the choice. When I sit in the dark now, and think about it, I know for certain that the life in between, and after, was well worth the fifty dollars and eleven years.

Rod G. Boriack

where to Begin?

- Each week try a wine from a different country. Start with the varietals from Down Under, next do a little California dreaming, then head over to Europe to enjoy the fruits of Germany, France, and Italy.

- Try whites, reds, rosés; Zinfandels, Bordeaux, Syrahs, Champagnes, and Beaujolais. When you do find something you like, try offerings from many different wineries.

- Record your impressions of each wine. How did it smell when you uncorked it? Was it thick or thin when you swirled it around your glass? How did it smell once poured? What did you taste? Don't worry about using sophisticated, flowery vocabulary—just make notes to yourself so you can remember what you liked or didn't enjoy.

- Ask questions of everyone you come in contact with: retailers, bartenders and waiters. If they're trained properly, they'll be able to help you make a good selection.

- See if your local wine store or restaurant offers wine flights. This gives you the opportunity to sample a half-dozen or so wines without having to purchase a glass or a bottle.

- Attend wine tastings designed for people just beginning to learn about wine.

A Thanksgiving Toast

Love wholeheartedly, be surprised,
give thanks and praise—then you will
discover the fullness of your life.

Brother David Steindl-Rast

T
he leaves had turned to a bright crimson and the premature nightfall brought with it a definite chill. I sat before the fireplace and inhaled the woodsy fragrance of charred oak. The cozy warmth of the scene was intoxicating. A good man (my husband of thirty years) sat beside me, in front of the romantic flames, leaving just one thing to complete this perfect evening. A glass of exquisite wine. But what fine wine could be worthy of this precious moment?

Coincidentally, preparations had begun for our Thanksgiving dinner. It would be a poignant time for all, as my son and his new wife were visiting for the first time since their wedding two years ago. Our daughters would be home, too, creating a family reunion of sorts. I desired everything to be perfect, yet was very aware that life is at best imperfect. Still, I was giving it my all. E-mails were sent to everyone asking what favored Thanksgiving comfort food was desired at the table. Judging by the responses,

I would be cooking for quite a while. Nevertheless, it gave me a thrill that they each had their very own favorite dish. Too bad that nothing but the turkey itself is a universal favorite.

They have also offered their favorite wines—Chardonnay, Pinot Grigio, Pinot Noir. I'll have these on hand, of course, but I yearn for something different. Something that is pleasant, loveable, and merry. A wine—either red, rosé, blush, or white—that is catchy and brimming with charisma. Something that reflects the joy of the season. What has been tasted in the past that could suit this occasion?

I think back to the few wine tasting sessions that my husband and I have been fortunate to attend. Two sessions were formal on cruise lines. However, our introduction to wine tasting occurred as newlyweds at our first neighborhood party in Minnesota. Each couple brought two bottles of predetermined wine and a complementary cheese. My husband and I were babes in the cradle, in our early twenties, as were every other couple in attendance. Eager to present ourselves as more than novices, we studied proper wine etiquette before the party. First of all, we read, you must look at the wine. Assess its color and clarity. My husband would pour the wine properly down the side of a goblet, raise it to eye level, and study the contents. At this point, I giggled. We were hardly wine snobs. We were beginners, peasants, commoners, young middle-class Americans trying not to embarrass ourselves. Then, together we would swirl the wine around the glass. This usually resulted in wine being hurled right out of the goblet, but I digress. The reason to swirl, it was revealed, is to oxygenate the wine, to release its aroma, to allow it to come alive. Smelling the wine, it states in our wine manual, "is half the fun of drinking it."

Thirty years ago, at this first read, my eyes rolled. Smelling wine is half the fun of drinking it? Get serious ... ah, youth and its impatience! Now I savor the importance of this step. To inhale the bouquet of a good wine must be like taking your first step into heaven. Sheer joy overtakes you. There is a promise of pure delight ahead! Ecstasy awaits! We never really perfected the step of properly sipping fine wine. It all seemed a bit pretentious to me. A delicate little sip, rolled about the tongue, held there and then spit out? Are you crazy? A fine wine costs a pretty penny. I don't gulp wine (anymore) but certainly won't spit it out. A small swig and a dainty swallow fills the bill, thank you very much. If you can't figure out if you like a wine by the swig-and-swallow method, then you are undeserving to imbibe. (Diana's rule.)

"Would you like some wine?" my husband asked. After thirty years you seem to develop a certain level of clairvoyance. Mind reading, anyway.

"There's a bottle in the refrigerator," I answered. He got up and retrieved the bottle while shaking his head.

"You never chill red wine," he said. Had I learned nothing over the years?

"Wrong, o wine connoisseur," I replied. "Beaujolais should be served slightly chilled."

"Beaujo what?"

"Beaujolais. It's a red wine from France's Beaujolais region. Made from Gamay grapes. We are trying Beaujolais

Villages. It's supposed to be fruity, exuberant and an intensely perfumed wine."

"Done your research, I see."

"It's a possibility for Thanksgiving. Beaujolais Villages. After this bottle we will try Beaujolais Nouveau, a fresh, young wine released each year on the third Thursday of November, hence, Thanksgiving wine."

"This is last year's," he said reading the label. 'Beaujolais is meant to be consumed very fresh—within the first four months to one year of release.' Hmm. Why?"

"The wine is made by a special process called carbonic maceration—fermenting entire bunches of grapes—to give it a bright, juicy flavor without the mouth-drying tannins of heavy red wines. It's best when fresh; can flatten with age. It's a good red, entry-level wine for white-wine partisans." I explained.

A Sensory Experience

Do you open a rich red wine and smell flowers? Perhaps they grew adjacent to, or in the same soil of the vineries in Spain or Italy. Does the taste of a Riesling evoke a taste of stone or minerals? No doubt it's due to the abundance of slate and limestone in the soil of German vineyards.

"Kind of like Kool-Aid."

I frown. "No, Beaujolais."

"You just like to say it," my husband kidded.

"I do," I answer. "Beaujolais, Beaujolais, Beaujolais. It's catchy, smart."

"And French."

"Oui, oui." My husband pours the Beaujolais Villages carefully into a crystal wine glass. He lifts it and examines the color and clarity. A gentle, experienced swirl released the fruity aroma of Gamay grapes. He sniffs the bouquet, and then takes a sip.

"Hmmm. Not bad," he says before giving me the wine goblet. I take it, chagrined. It's a bad habit of his to taste-test from my glass. "Beaujo what?" he asks again as he pours his own glass.

"Beaujolais," I say with a grin. "Now you're just teasing."

"I just like to hear you say it," he replied while giving me a fruity kiss. He sat down beside me in front of the now roaring fire. We clicked our glasses in a satisfied salute. "Happy Thanksgiving," I say snuggling next to him. "We have found our dinner wine." And we sipped Beaujolais as the fire crackled and danced before us.

Diana M. Amadeo

No Good Thing

The most important thing a father can do for
his children is to love their mother.

David O. McKay

T hey called it "Bourelje." I hated it as a kid. Stupid tradition. Every single day my parents had to have *their* time. Dad would get home from work, Mom would pour a glass of wine, and together they would sit and talk about the day. This was their "Bourelje hour." Both from the Netherlands, they claimed it was some type of Dutch tradition to strengthen their marriage.

My four older brothers and I didn't buy it. We knew it was more than that—a clandestine meeting to discuss punishments, a strategy meeting on teaching us "responsibility for our own good." Surely that was closer to the truth. We kids weren't even allowed in the room. Depending on the day, we would overhear bits and pieces of conversation. Sometimes they'd laugh out loud, other times we'd hear the rhythm of deep exchanges or sometimes it was so quiet, we'd wonder if they were whispering about whether to even keep us for another day. It was nearly torturous when we would overhear our own name . . . and then nothing else but muffled frustration.

♟ The Yin and Yang of Wine

Sweetness and acidity complement each other. A sweet wine needs acidity to avoid becoming syrupy, and an acidic wine needs some sweetness to temper the sourness. The longer grapes stay on the vine, the sweeter they become, and the less acid remains. Grape growers try to harvest their crop when the decreasing acids and increasing sugars reach a balance.

No good, we collectively thought, can come from such things.

We were wrong.

Boatloads of good came from such things. Fifty years of marriage. Five grown, independent, and productive kids. Twelve grandkids with growing hopes and dreams of their own.

I now have my own Bourelje time. When my husband comes home, I pour him a glass of wine and gather a few snacks. We hide away from the children, shut the door, and toast the day. Sometimes we spend fifteen minutes, more often we spend an hour, talking through the day, discussing the kids, sharing our lives.

Our kids hate it. They wonder what we're up to. They squirm when they hear their own names. They call out, "No good thing can come from this!" And my husband and I giggle to each other, take another sip of wine, and toast every good thing that has so sweetly come from *this*.

Elsa Kok Colopy

Varietals are the spice of life!

Opposites Attract

*The only thing that you can carry
with you on your travels is your heart.
So fill your heart with good things,
and good things will follow you
for the rest of your life.*

Scott Murray

"Y ou are the one with the class," my boyfriend
always told me. I was twenty-nine. He was forty-
five. I was living a bohemian life in Manhattan.
He lived on an estate in upstate New York. I had traveled
throughout greater Europe and North Africa on five dollars a day, sleeping in youth hostels or camping out on
luggage racks on overnight train rides. His idea of rough-
ing it was downgrading to a four-star hotel. I had been
arrested for nude sunbathing in Cinque Terre, Italy. He
had never skinny-dipped. So I took him to the nude
beaches of French St. Maarten. I may have had some class,
learned perhaps from books, movies, and observation of
others in my travels, but he had a budget far greater than
anything I had ever seen. Yet, with all of that money, he
still wanted to see the world through my eyes.

He was intrigued by my involvement with wine. He

suggested that we travel together to visit some of my favorite wine destinations. We ended up a few months later in one of the most famous vineyards of the world, Domaine de la Romanée-Conti, in the Côte d'Or, in Burgundy, France.

I was awestruck by the simplicity of it. It was just a vineyard, like many others I had seen before. Sure, this was a prime site with more than two centuries of history. But there were rows of vines, with dirt in between them, and a modest little stone gate with the great name etched into it. That was it.

We drove right up to the gate, parked, and stepped freely right into the vineyards. We were completely alone. As far as we knew, we were not being observed. I couldn't imagine that anyone could just waltz in like this, but there we were, and I was speechless.

I was so engrossed in my surroundings, bending down to observe the clusters of precious grapes, touching the vines, examining the shoots, digging my toes in the soil, that I didn't even notice what my dear friend was up to. I heard the sound of water, and thought, then turned around, and, utterly horrified, watched as my soon-to-be-ex-boyfriend finished taking a whiz right onto a vine, after which he pronounced, "This year's harvest will be even better now!"

That night, we ambled into a friendly-looking Auberge St. Vincent in the town of Beaune, a central hub and a great base for exploring Burgundy. The restaurant was named after the Patron Saint of Burgundy. Even though our palates were fatigued—we had visited five properties

℞ Priceless vinegar

Thomas Jefferson, a philosopher, ambassador to France, and the third president of the United States, was a winemaker and collector. Bottles in his collection were etched with the initials "Th. J." A bottle of his 1787 Bordeaux, Château Lafite, sold for $160,000 in 1985, long after it had turned sour and undrinkable.

that day—I was still feeling like a kid in a candy store. I couldn't wait to see what gems we might find on that wine list. But before I even had a chance to open it, my now-for-sure-soon-to-be-ex-boyfriend said to the waiter, "Bring us a couple of Heinekens. We've had enough of your wine around here." The waiter's expression mirrored my own, though my skin was the shade of a fiery red beet.

A hush fell over the entire room. Even the non-French were looking down their noses at us and thinking, "What an insult! What crass behavior! Mon dieu!" I wanted to crawl into a cave and never come out.

Was I upset? Yes. Was I humiliated? You bet.

Hmm. Come to think of it, I suppose that is how my friend felt as he stared, standing in water up to his waist unencumbered by swim trunks, at the shoreline of that nude beach in St. Maarten. I had egged him on to take off his shorts and go for a swim. I had promised to apply sunscreen anywhere on his body he so desired when he came back, knowing that I had a bottle of spray-on lotion in my bag. It was early, and only a few stragglers were on the beach, so he went for it. By now, however, several families with small children had arrived, and he was absolutely mortified. He begged and pleaded, as I stood fully clad in my bathing suit on the shore, taunting him.

I wonder, now, looking back on that glorious day, how long he had been plotting his revenge.

Catherine Fallis

The Makings of a Sommelier

Wine is bottled poetry.

Robert Louis Stevenson

Recently my husband and I decided to explore California wines by attending a local wine society event held at a hotel in Irvine. Arriving at the parking lot, we made our way, round and round, up and up, ramp after ramp behind a stream of cars spewing nasty exhaust. Level after level, there was not a single parking space to be found. Arriving at the top level, we were greeted by obviously bored parking lot attendants who motioned us to the end, where we managed to squeeze between a BMW and a Hummer.

Adapting the herd mentality, we scurried through the garage to the elevator through the lobby, and up an escalator where we found ourselves at the registration table. I took a closer look at the people we'd be spending as much as three hours with. There was a tall woman wearing a battery-powered flashing pendant in the shape of a wine glass. Another sported massive, sparkling wine clusters dangling from her ear lobes. Men wore Hawaiian-style shirts printed with grape vines and wine bottles. And most everyone had a special plastic plate that was square with a corner cut out to hold a wine glass, leaving one hand free.

Caught up in the community of it all, I determined that before tasting any fruit of the vine or savoring a single morsel, I must have a plastic plate. Not to have one made us painfully stand out as the wine rookies we are. I told my husband of twenty years my concern. Recognizing my countenance he took my arm and ushered me through the long corridor to the ballroom side-entry. Turning his head from right to left scanning the room, he spotted where to buy the plates. He left. He returned. And now with my plate I could swagger through the aisles with the best of them.

Skimming the list of over 100 different wineries, I didn't recognize a single one. It could have rattled me, but I was able to call on my inner actress so as not to appear the least bit a wine society newbie.

Aisle after aisle, glistening whites and enticing reds beckoned us. I sauntered over to the booth where a handsome man stood describing the microclimate regions within his vineyard to another who sipped the seductive fruit of the vine. The two men seemed well acquainted.

I learned that the handsome man was also the vintner as he offered me a sampling, of Pinot Noir. Holding my glass up to the fluorescent overhead lights, I swirled it. I brought it to my face and lowered my nose into it, breathing deeply to identify the subtleties. I tasted. The handsome man keenly searched my face for signs of pleasure, his mouth partially open wanting to speak, but daring not to. The man standing next to me couldn't wait, and abruptly asked, "Well, what do you think?" The question shocked me out of my pleasurable wine tasting induced daze.

Oh no, I thought, *I'm being asked to critique the wine!* I can't possibly look at my flavor wheel now or my rookie status will be revealed. Searching my mind for words that I remembered others used when commenting on this varietal, I finally spoke. "Jammy." The handsome man's eyes widened as his posture heightened and a triumphant smile transformed his face. "You have a good palette," he said. The man standing next to me readily agreed. Smiling wryly I thought, I deserve an Oscar.

Knowing that one is only as good as one's last performance, I started to walk away but the vintner stopped me. "Wait, I want you to try this." He poured what was the last sampling of a dark Malbec—a wine I'd never tried before. The man standing next to me cried out, "She got the last of it? I haven't tasted any yet." His expression betrayed his attempt to sound like he was teasing. "Well, then you'll at least have to tell me what it tastes like."

Oh, no, not again! I felt the sick sense of panic rising within me. Not wanting the nervous shaking of my hands to give me away, I stabilized my glass on the table to swirl. I turned my face away to conceal my anxiety. Raising the glass to my nose, I breathed appreciably and intentionally made noise as I sipped, drawing in air—buying time while trying to maintain my image. "Well?" the vintner anxiously inquired.

I remained silent for the longest time knowing the fewer words I spoke the better, lest I blow my image as a seasoned connoisseur.

With the residual tannins tantalizing my tongue, I blurted out "Young." The vintner all but applauded me and elatedly looked to his friend saying, "She has an excellent palette! It's only been bottled for two weeks." And with that I tipped my head and my glass, smiled pretty, and walked away imitating the feminine swagger of Merle Steep.

Radiating confidence over my performance, I walked over to my husband who was sampling duck confete. Strolling over to the next aisle with our plastic pates prominently displayed as a symbol that we belonged, I said to my husband, "You know honey I'm pretty certain that I have what it takes to become a distinguished sommelier." Refusing to be fazed by his eye rolling, I suggested we make plans for the upcoming Paso Robles Wine Festival. He quipped, "Then we'd better start memorizing more descriptions from the flavor wheel."

 Taste Test

Pinot Noir boasts cherry and raspberry flavors.

Syrah or *Shiraz* grapes produce a spicy, deep, rich full-bodied wine.

Muscadet and *Verdicchio* grapes generally make good dry, crisp whites.

Sauvignon Blanc is tangy and zesty.

A blend of *Sémillon* and *Sauvignon Blanc* produces a rich, nuttier-flavored white.

Chardonnay lends itself to a ripe, tropical fruit flavor.

Rosés, from the Grenache grape, are fragrant and refreshing.

He can be such a chump at times. Just the same, I determined that we'd be attending the Zin Fest; after all, I've clearly discovered my new role in life.

Pamela Christian

From Jug to Cork

Age appears to be best in four things—
old wood best to burn, old wine to drink, old
friends to trust, and old authors to read.

Sir Francis Bacon

With each birthday, the years seem to swirl around me faster and faster, like I'm standing in a tornado. The same winds of time that took my hair, unkindly left a few extra pounds around the middle. My body now snap-crackle-and-pops when I bend my knees, and my shoes suddenly seem too far away when laces are undone. But biology is only one measurement. As I march through time, something else changes: the wine at my table.

I was young once. Youth means energy, optimism, and the excitement of What's Next. It also means poverty. The first years of our marriage were burdened with a stack of unpaid bills that remained high when the paycheck was gone. In the poor years of my youth, there was jug wine— three gallons for three bucks. When you're young and poor, the taste buds haven't matured. During those years, my taste buds were still excited to be allowed alcohol. "Fine wine" meant chilled. If the Chablis was cold, then it was good.

I had strapped on a few more years before discovering box wine. Box wine, in our mind, was a little more "high brow." A local winery, well respected in the industry, sold a four-liter box of Chardonnay that was heaven. More expensive than jugs, it was still reasonably priced. Even better, I felt clever when I learned that another two glasses could be squeezed from the plastic bag long after the slurping sound from the nozzle suggested the box was dry. Regardless, my Life Buddy and I were excited to move up the social rung.

By the time our children were in high school, we could afford wine with corks—at least on the weekends. The two of us celebrated the end of a long week by sitting around the pool, scoring our children in an endless competition of cannon balls and hand stands, with wine glasses in hand. We learned to treasure the pop of the cork screw, and tried to hide our disappointment when Monday rolled around and the box was pulled from the fridge.

My wife and I now have a century between us, two grown children, four grandchildren, and a bump in a tummy that's promised to be number five. The mirror isn't as kind anymore. What hair that's left is more gray than blond. Young men call me "sir," and I feel compelled to share my wisdom with whoever will listen.

But the graph that charts our age climbing high over the years also shows a salary growth that supports memberships in as many wine clubs as we have grandchildren. My fridge hasn't seen a wine box since Bill Clinton walked the halls of the White House. I now have a dedicated wine fridge in the laundry room for the Chardonnay, a wine cabinet from Bombay in the dining room for the Cabernets, and a filled wine rack in the garage for the overflow.

From jug to cork, life is good.

David R. Wilkins

A Show Stopper

For thousands of years, cork has served the wine industry as a stopper for vintages young and old.

Cork is made from the bark of the cork oak tree (*Quercus suber*), an evergreen whose unique, light-gray bark develops very thick layers of cork, ridged and furrowed, and reddish brown when harvested.

High-quality oaks used in winemaking have a very fine grain, with few faults. The cork is dried until only 5 to 8 percent moisture is retained, which allows it to be compressed. A faulty cork can cause the wine to smell moldy or musty. Many winemakers moved to the use of synthetic corks, which reduces the incidence of spoilage.

In 2004 the Vino-Seal™ debuted. Developed by Alcoa Closures Systems, the glass stopper, which resembles a crystal decanter, uses an inert o-ring to hermetically seal each bottle. The innovative, patented design prevents oxidation and contaminates from entering the bottle, while maintaining desired levels of free sulfur. As an added bonus, no corkscrew is needed and the wine can be resealed with the same stopper. After only two years on the market, Vino-Seal had been selected by nearly 500 wineries worldwide as the stopper of choice for their premium wines.

A Box of Wine

Wine adds soul to a new memory.

Author Unknown

Moonlight streamed around the dense clouds, but paled in comparison to the thousands of stars that sparkled in the night sky. It never ceased to amaze my husband, Tazz, or me how bright it always was at night above that house. Despite living in a city, the stars always shined brightly and the sunrises and sunsets were awe inspiring. But as beautiful as the sunsets were, it was the stars that pulled us outside with our box of wine each night.

A box of wine! A box, you may be thinking. Yes, a box. Though the type of wine varied from Chablis, to Sunset Blush, to Burgundy, to chillable red, the brand was always Franzia. Tazz convinced me very quickly that boxed wines were the most underestimated in the world of wines. "The red-headed stepchild of wines," he would jokingly say.

Like every other night, we sipped wine and talked about whatever came to mind. Some of our conversations were silly—like creating a pocket book of outlandish jokes—and some of our conversations were serious. We talked about elections and politics, Roman and Arcadian history, and many other topics that sprang to mind. Those days, sitting on the porch and watching the stars, are still some of my favorite memories with my husband.

What caught my eye on this particular night was not the stars in the sky or the beautiful way the clouds shrouded the moon. It was the twinkle I saw in his eyes as he looked at me. There was not a doubt in my mind that his heart was as filled with joy and love for me as mine was for him.

The thought of losing him—whether it be that night or in fifty years—tore at my heart, clenched my throat, and brimmed my eyes with tears. Nothing in the world would ever replace him. My handsome husband. Light of my heart.

As a matter of fact, I knew that should anything happen to him, I would die of a broken heart. Why the thoughts filled my head as he stared so lovingly into my eyes, I will never know.

As if reading my mind, Tazz—my loving, wonderful husband—placed his glass of wine on the ground at his feet and put his arms around me. His embrace was not too tight, but not loose either. He held me in his comforting embrace and kissed my cheek.

"All of the beautiful sunsets and stars in the sky hold no weight in their beauty compared to you," he whispered into my ear. "I love you more than anything else. You are my sun, moon, and stars all wrapped up in one. My heart. I will do everything in my power to stay with you as long as God permits me, and I will never leave you. I promise you that."

I tried my best to swallow the fear and gave him a kiss to ensure him that I understood and returned the feelings.

When Tazz and I first married—after four months of dating—everyone told us we rushed into it too fast. Most of them had little faith in the strength of our marriage. Sitting on the porch that night I laughed to myself as I took another sip of my cool wine. Most of those friends who doubted our love and commitment had drifted away from us. If only they could see us at that moment, staring into each others eyes under the stars. We were so filled with love that the world would have had to be blind not to see it.

Though our marriage has grown in many ways since those nights on that porch, I still miss that house and the memories we made every night with nothing but our love, the stars, and a box of wine.

Star Davies

Bag in a Box

Driven by convenience and consumer demand, wine packaged in bag-in-box containers is becoming more popular worldwide.

Unlike bottles, which once opened allow air to contact the wine, the bag-in-box contracts as the volume of wine inside decreases. It prevents contact with the air, and the quality of the taste is retained.

A flexible bag and oxygen barrier films are connected to a spout and enclosed in a cardboard box. Holding from two to twenty litres, no corkscrew is required, and the bag-in-box is easily transported.

No longer associated with cheap wines, this concept has been adopted by upscale wine producers for their more expensive wines, and have made the significant investment it takes to buy a full bag-in-box packaging line, the largest of which can fill several million bags.

Share This Wine with Me!

The world is a great book;
he who never stirs from home,
reads only a page.

Saint Augustine

On vacation in Spain in the early 1990s, we met a lovely young couple from Belgium. Interested in learning about our national customs, they plied us with questions about Scottish traditions and habits, but we were a disappointment to Ann and Koen right from the start. Contrary to the stereotypical Scot, neither my husband, Eric, nor I drinks whisky. Rather, we prefer red wine. When they learned that we did not eat bacon and eggs for breakfast, and actually preferred coffee, we knew that we had let them down again.

The four of us dined together regularly, and usually enjoyed a couple of bottles of wine with our meal; Ann and Koen preferred white, Eric and I our customary red.

One day, while enjoying an outdoor lunch by the pool, we chose a bottle from a local vineyard neither Eric nor I recognized. Feeling adventurous and anticipating the delight in unraveling the mysteries of an unfamiliar varietal, Eric started to pour when nothing happened. Confused and with some anguish, he said, "It's no comin' oot!" in full Scottish accent.

Now, normally when speaking with our friends we spoke in proper English, but Eric had said this without thinking. I glanced at the bottle, took it from him, unscrewed the cap, and just smiled. We always drink Italian or French wine in corked bottles and this was our first encounter with a screw-on top. Feeling a bit of an idiot in front of our friends, but pleased that I was not going to call further attention to his faux pas, Eric leaned over, picked up my hand and kissed it. Ann and Koen smiled at the gesture. Our lunch proceeded uneventfully, filled with delicious food, the company of new friends, and a red that did not disappoint; it was full-bodied and quite enjoyable.

A few days later, when the four of us again met for lunch. Koen picked up their bottle of wine, frowned at it, and said what sounded like "Isno Kumminoot." Ann smiled at him, leaned over, and unscrewed the top. Koen then picked up her hand and kissed it. For an instant, we assumed they were having a go at imitating us as a joke.

Koen smiled as he poured their wine. "We speak at night, and we like very much this Scottish custom, to open the wine for each other and kiss the hand. We think it is very romantic. What does "Isno Kummin oot!" mean?"

Eric and I glanced at each other, and Eric instantly replied, "Oh, it's an old Gaelic saying for, 'open this wine for me and I will share my love with you!'" I grinned back at Ann and Koen and kicked Eric hard on the ankle under the table, another Scottish custom they probably didn't know about.

Joyce Stark

Generations of Quality

In 1927, a group of fifty-two grape growers in the town of Lerga, located in the Navarra region of northern Spain, took a dramatic step and united behind a local priest. They formed a consortium to buy back the land of Lerga, the majority of which was owned by a local noble family, headed by the Count of Guendulain.

Each of the fifty-two growers were given equal parcels of the vineyards to run, work, and tend themselves. Since 1927, the grape growers in Lerga have taken enormous pride in the fact that they own and manage the vineyards that they purchased with their own sweat and toil.

The grandchildren of these growers still continue the legacy of the now 60- to 100-year-old vines.

Bodegas Bernabe Navarro 2003 Beryna from Alicante is one of the most delicious red wines from the Navarra region. *Wine Enthusiast* rates it a 90, and describes it as a "complex winner that smells like dark cherries and tastes like a swirl of raspberry, plum, and chocolate." Mmmm, what more could you want!

If you fancy a white from Spain, try CVNE 2005 Monopole, from the Rioja region. It's fresh and fruity with a floral aroma with flavors of melon, banana, and papaya.

To Wine ... or Not to Wine

When one has tea and wine
one will have many friends.

Chinese proverb

T
hat was the question. It just seemed appropriate. A glass of wine to celebrate life's simple things: our favorite lunch spot and a small slice of time carved out of two busy friends' lives. We weren't able to meet for lunch very often. Our careers and family demands seemed to crowd out the ability to do so. Becky and I had an understanding about scheduling lunch. If, at the last minute, one of us was forced to cancel due to some unforeseen conflict, no explanation or justification was required. After several attempts to meet, we finally found a mutually agreeable time, and wine with Italian cuisine seemed like the perfect way to celebrate a scheduling coup!

Still, there was our professional image to consider. She was in insurance; I was in banking. Neither of us wanted to take the chance of being seen with wine over lunch and having the scene misconstrued by some other diner. The prudent thing was to nix the wine idea all together. It did not seem fair, but we were women, living in a conservative world. Fair or not, people were held to certain standards.

Fortunately, some of us operate on creativity. As Lupé, our favorite waiter, jotted down my meal order, I added nonchalantly, "I'd also like a glass of Merlot. In a coffee cup." This request caught Becky off guard. Lupé's pen stopped in its tracks. He raised his eyebrows and a small smile of understanding crept onto his face. Becky added a glass to the order as well. Then I asked, "Surely, we're not the first ones to ever request wine in a coffee cup, are we?" Lupé raised his eyebrows again. We took that as a "yes." I didn't think my idea was *that* creative. Our dilemma apparently was solved. If Becky and I could've slapped each other with a high five across the table at that moment, we would have.

🍷 *Glass or plastic?*

The French are some of the most traditional purists in the wine world, yet have always had the option of buying wine in *en vrac*. Plastic jugs in hand, locals show up at a merchant or château and get refilled by tap from a large vat.

Lupé reappeared shortly with our two cups of "coffee." A spoon rested on each saucer. Nice touch. As he set the cups and saucers down, he cautioned us, "Very hot! Very hot!" Our partner in crime was nothing short of brilliant. We all laughed, appreciating his efforts to honor our discretion. Becky leaned over to look in my cup; then looked into hers and asked, "Did you order Merlot for a reason?"

"Yes. It's dark. Like coffee."

"Good idea," Becky lamented. "Your Merlot really does look like coffee. My Zinfandel, on the other hand, looks more like Easter-egg dye."

Indeed it did, but we refused to let the pallor of her coffee dampen our spirits and small victory. In Europe, our concern for being seen with wine at lunch would be admonished. In Monterrey, Manhattan, or on Michigan Avenue, we would have been rushed to a self-esteem support group. But in Middle America, alcohol is still equated with the clock. It's always happy hour somewhere, but the level of discretion will always differ for some of us. But now, at least, when the question arises for our beverage order, we have the freedom to answer, "Coffee, tea, or *vino!*

Bobbe White

The Greatest Vintage

*Friendship is the only cement that
will hold the world together.*

Winston Churchill

At about 5:30 each evening, while the sun is still high in the Connecticut sky, my girlfriend Susan calls me from her home just two miles away. By that time, our collective six children are settled down in front of the television, and our husbands have left their offices and are commuting home for the evening. Dinners are cooking in our respective ovens, and Susan and I can toast the end of another successful day with a glass of Pinot in our hands. We use the more endearing term "Pinot" because we consider the variety a close friend. A friend who is going to quietly support us as we whittle away the day's tension.

"Got your glass?" Susan asks when I answer the call.

"Clink, clink," I say in return, signaling that I'm ready. Our hectic day of parenting is coming to an end; reinforcements are on their way (and hopefully won't get stuck in traffic). We carefully tap our glasses against our handset receivers and start to gab. Susan's voice warms me more than any amount of alcohol settling in my system. I love being able to commiserate with an empathetic soul about the hardest and poorest-paying job on earth.

We both have three children, all under the age of eight, and each day brings new challenges of potty training, disciplining, educating . . . After ten hours of nonstop parenting, this is one break we consistently give ourselves. It's not dependent upon the weather, or our babysitting budget; the only requirements for this nightly routine are that we are both in our homes with nowhere to go, our kids are safely occupied, and we have a bottle of Pinot on hand.

The first few sips are spaced between sentences that are full of tension. "If one more kid calls my name, I'm gonna lose it!" Susan might say one afternoon. "They're driving me crazy, all three of them!" I might say on another.

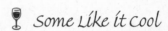 Some Like it Cool

Pinot Gris (Pinto Grigio in Italy) and Pinot Noir are versatile wines. They range from fresh and crisp to rich and creamy. Cooler climates, like Oregon, offer ideal growing conditions for Pinot. Most Oregon wine regions lie in valleys between the southern Cascade Mountains and the coast.

After breaking the ice, we talk our way through the day's events and unpack the deeper baggage we don't want to carry with us into tomorrow. Like the time my five-year-old son, Alexander, kissed one of his female classmates *on the lips;* we worked through what needed to be done, and then giggled like schoolgirls. Or when my seven-year-old son, Nicholas, told me he no longer wanted to kiss me in the mornings outside the elementary school doors. Susan cried in her glass, just as I did, at the reality that our babies will grow up too fast.

With each sip of Pinot, our baggage gets lighter and lighter. By the end of a single glass, we're both in a new place. When my two-year-old daughter, Gianna, comes into the kitchen wanting a drink of water, I whisper, "Of course, sweetheart," and I get one for her with a smile while listening to Susan's plans for the rest of her evening.

By the time our husbands get home from work we realize we don't need them to relieve us after all. Thanks to a special white grape from Italy, the witching hour in our homes is actually enchanted. But the magic wand that creates the enchantment in our lives? It's friendship, the greatest vintage around.

Karen M. Lynch

Champagne and Fortune Cookies

Wine awakens and refreshes
lurking passions of the mind, as varnish
does the colors of a picture and brings
them out in all their natural glowings.

Alexander Pope

After a short courtship, Bob and I realized we were in love. Since each of us treasured our friends, we wanted them to get to know each other. To make the introduction a special occasion, we invited them to my home for a homemade Chinese dinner. I spent all day preparing egg rolls, almond boneless chicken, fried rice, and Madam Wo's delicious shredded chicken salad. I even prepared a steamed, sponge rice cake with mandarin orange sauce for dessert.

That evening our friends arrived, and each brought us a thank-you gift. Bob's friends brought wine—one couple a Chablis and the other, Champagne. My friends arrived with a small tray of fortune cookies. I was delighted, not having thought of it myself.

The meal went well, the wine enjoyed, and as I cleared the dishes to present my dessert, I thought about the Champagne. I asked Bob to bring the bottle to the table, but before he opened it, Bernice asked if it was time for the fortune cookies?

"Great," I said, and as I sliced the cake, she walked around with the tray of cookies while each person opened theirs, laughing at the messages inside. I was the last to receive mine, and I set it on my plate.

Bob pointed to the cookie. "Aren't you going to read your fortune?"

It seemed important to him, so I broke the cookie and pulled out the narrow slip of paper. "This house will be filled with happiness," I read, looking around the room at our wonderful blend of friends. "That's really nice," I said.

I broke off a hunk and nibbled on it as Bob watched me. I sensed he wanted me to do something or say something, but I was at a loss.

We watched as Bob removed the wrapper and loosened the cork on the bottle of Champagne. With a fizz and loud thwack, the cork flew into the air and bounced off the ceiling, leaving a small dark indentation in the plaster. We laughed and waited as Bob poured the Champagne into fluted glasses. Before anyone could make the toast, I felt something hard in the corner of my fortune cookie. "Something's in this," I exclaimed, dropping it to the table.

All eyes were on me as I stared at the piece of white tissue hanging from the slit of my cookie. Bob leaned closer. "What is it?"

"I don't know." My stomach churning at the thought of what might be inside. Chewed gum? Worse?

"Open it."

Fearing something disgusting was inside, I reluctantly

tugged out the tissue and unfolded it. A beautiful solitaire diamond ring fell into my hand. I held it up for everyone to see, stunned at it being in my cookie. "Someone lost a ring in this cookie!" I muttered.

Everyone talked at once, but Bob laughed and shook his head. "It's an engagement ring." I gazed at him grinning from ear to ear. "It's my engagement ring," he repeated. Finally I caught on.

Only Bob and Bernice were in on the surprise. The rest of our friends were as astonished as I was, and most women had tears rolling down their cheeks. I looked from Bob to my friend and back. "When did you do this? How?" Only having met Bernice a couple of times, I couldn't imagine how he accomplished this feat.

🍷 Humble Beginnings

Dom Pierre Pérignon, a blind Benedictine monk, discovered the wine now known as champagne. As the chief cellar master at Hautvillers he perfected the technique for its production and bottled the first bottle of champagne in 1668. Centuries later, Dom Pérignon is one of the finest champagnes in the world.

"Let's have a toast," someone said. The answer to my question sailed away as everyone lifted their glasses to wish us a lifetime of happiness. At that moment, I remembered the strip of paper in the cookie—"this house will be filled with happiness."

The fortune cookie spoke the truth, but God made it possible. He has truly filled this house with happiness. A few years later, when it was time to paint the dining room, I looked up at the dark spot still visible on the ceiling and was saddened by the thought of it being gone.

Bob tackled the paint job, and a couple days later when I found the courage to look up at the ceiling, my heart did a dance. He'd painted around that tiny spot. When I let out a cry, he came into the room to see what had happened.

I pointed to the ceiling. "You left the spot." He only grinned, then drew me into his arms and kissed me. After twenty-two years, the spot is still on the ceiling and happiness still fills this house.

Gail Gaymer Martin

The Secret Ingredient

I cook with wine; sometimes
I even add it to the food.

W.C. Fields

My mother is an amazing cook whose talents would put Martha Stewart to shame. As a twelve-year-old I was keen to emulate her culinary skills. One day, I decided to make a leg of lamb for dinner, which my mother bought, impressed that I would tackle such a feat alone. My mother left me, confident that she would not regret a night off from cooking. We agreed that the fact that I prepared the lamb would be our secret.

I was so excited and thought hard about my marinade. I decided that a bottle of red wine would be an excellent addition to the many other added flavors. I snuck down to the basement and made a beeline to the wine buffet that my father made by hand, sometime before he was twenty years old. Despite my sneaky behavior, I shuffled through every bottle of wine, checking all of the dates, so that I could find the least desirable bottle out of collection. I finally chose the oldest bottle of wine from some foreign land I could not pronounce, and knew my father would appreciate my calculated and thoughtful choice.

I snuck back up the stairs into the kitchen, positive no one had ever thought of my very clever, secret ingredient before. From years of observation, I learned that uncorking a bottle of wine was not difficult at all. I poured the entire bottle into the pan, added my onion, garlic, and spices, and the smell was intoxicating. I snuck back downstairs to sneak a shot of bourbon into my marinade. I was incredibly mature, after all, cooking with wine—and not the kind of wine made for cooking. I chopped and stirred the marinade around the leg of lamb until I was happy with the rich melody of smells parading through my nostrils. I covered the leg with foil and placed it in the refrigerator.

My mother actually cooked the leg of lamb and the other parts of the meal as well. At twelve years old, however, I was convinced that my preparation of the lamb was indeed cooking the entire meal, entirely alone. All I wanted was to see my father's face as he tasted the leg of lamb. The suspense almost killed me, for as children, the one thing my siblings and I competed for the most was the approval from our father.

My father was absolutely amazed at the taste of the lamb, and was not sure what the meat was. I saw this as an unforeseen bonus, stumping my truly brilliant father. Even more exciting than I imagined, my siblings were inhaling the meat and asking for more. At an age when we seriously did not like each other at all this was a real coup. I told my father that it was lamb, which was something he would not have guessed. He tasted each bite with purpose, and finally he asked what the meat was marinated in. My mother shrugged and exposed the truth that I prepared the lamb.

I told my father about the onions, garlic, spices, and then with added uppity perk, I told him about the Jack Daniels, proud of my originality. He nodded, impressed, chewing thoughtfully, identifying in his mind each ingredient I spoke of. Finally my father observed, "No, there is something else . . . hmmm . . . did you use wine in the marinade?" Once again proving that there is nothing, not one thing, that his children could ever slide by him without notice, my siblings looked at me for confirmation. Stunned for a moment, I finally answered, "Uh . . . yes. Yes! There is wine in the marinade!"

My father asked me how much wine I used, and I was back in the game of eagerly talking about my cooking prowess. I told my father how I snuck down to his wine buffet and didn't pick just any bottle, but picked the oldest bottle in fear that it might've been spoiled because it was so old. He asked me the year, and I told him. But not to worry because I was smart, I smelled it first, and it smelled like the wine I would smell at holiday meals, so I knew it was okay to use. I even uncorked it all by myself. I was so proud and excited that I hadn't noticed that my father's fork never reached his mouth.

My father set his fork down, and calmly asked, "You used the whole bottle?" My smile quickly faded, not sure what was wrong.

"Uh, yes, Dad, I did," not sure how this was a bad thing.

My father asked, "You didn't leave enough, say, for a small glass that I might enjoy with the meal?"

"No, sir. I poured the whole bottle into the bowl."

He nodded, and stared briefly at his plate. My mother seemed confused as well, as my father only drank milk at dinner unless it was a special occasion with guests.

"Well, then. I think I'll eat some more lamb."

Finally, my father leaned back in his chair and sighed, patting his belly and proclaimed that the lamb was excellent. I was so proud, but still felt uneasy and not certain why. My father asked to see the empty bottle of wine, which I pulled out of the trash as my siblings ran off excused from the table. My father seemed happy and content digesting his meal, but I was still wary, and reluctantly I handed him the bottle. He looked at it and laughed. He laughed hard, gazing fondly at the label.

My father turned to me, holding the bottle in his hands, label side out so that I could see it plainly. He explained to me, at a level that a sixth grader could understand, the basics of wine, and in his explanation I learned that I had chosen his most expensive bottle of wine. My father invited me down to the basement where he explained how his wines were organized. I listened intently, trying to understand that some years were good years, and some bottles, though also very old, were not made in good years and therefore not as good as a younger wine. What I understood most of all, was that I was allowed to cook with wine, but under two conditions.

First, I must ask my father permission so that he may pick the bottle, for after all, not all wines go with all meats. And second, never ever use the whole bottle, for whatever wine I use from my father's collection, my father would like a couple of glasses from the same bottle to enjoy with the meal. I gladly shook on that deal.

Today, I find that not adding what I am drinking to whatever meat I am cooking is a sin. And through the years, I have learned that wine is an art not relegated to the kitchen. Wine must be chosen as thoughtfully as the company one chooses. It is the perfect compliment to a great friend. Like a steadfast friendship. And as I get older, I realize that my oldest friends are actually my siblings, who have been under my nose the whole time. The stories of our parental fear, our childhood

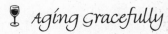 *Aging Gracefully*

Red wines are generally aged in barrels. Whites or rosés, if aged, are done so in a stainless steel tank, except for Chardonnay, which is aged in oak barrels.

home, those who have shared our dinner table, and of course, the glorious hard-won victories of torture and sibling combat, are more vivid and grander with every cork we pop.

Let there always be more laughter, and let there always be a glass of wine to help us remember to give thanks for all of the good moments in our lives. Salute!

Kathleen A. Alcorn

Apricots and Vermentino

Certainly, travel is more than
the seeing of sights; it is a change
that goes on, deep and permanent,
in the ideas of living.

Miriam Beard

Signorina Marina checked us into our rental apartment in the cliff-top complex she owned with her brother, and as she completed the paperwork, waved toward the window and her brilliant stretch of the Italian Riviera. She gave us our key. And two bottles of wine.

One red, one white, in unlabeled plastic carafes with tiddlywinkish stoppers. Language is no barrier in communicating the truly essential—which anything involving wine is—and our Engle-Italian exchange established that this was literal house wine, made on the premises from grapes grown on the premises. We'd seen the vines climbing the slope next to the driveway and crawling the arbors erected as sun screens over the parking lot and bocce court. Our check-in bottles were complimentary. When we emptied them, we were to bring them to reception, where they'd be refilled for about three dollars. Welcome to paradise.

We turned the key in the door of our unit and paradise got better. We found ourselves in a sun-filled aerie with a tiled terrace that hung over the Mediterranean. Below us, mahogany boats skipped over silver waves while thin people browned themselves atop rocks that poked from the sea. Vineyards, orchards, and olive groves marched up every mountainside, and Moneglia—a medieval hamlet turned tourist town—buzzed with beachgoers, shoppers, and café lingerers. There was no reason to move. We could take in this whole sun-drenched swath of the world from our hilltop perch.

My husband, Mike, and I quickly fell into a routine of sitting, sipping, staring, and little else. Our kids, Adam and Dana, explored the complex and its grounds, and polished their ping pong skills, often playing with a German girl on holiday with her parents. Their unit sat behind ours and looked onto the parking lot and ping pong table. In Moneglia on a month-long stay, they'd chosen to economize and forego the sea view.

We made short work of Signorina Marina's free check-in bottles and, while we enjoyed the red, it was the white we presented most to reception for refills. Pressed from Vermentino grapes that grow in the steep, sea-kissed vineyards that arc from Genoa southeast to Santa Margherita Ligure—an arc that includes Moneglia and Signorina Marina's family vineyards—the wine's crisp kick partnered perfectly with the slice of sultry dolce vita we feasted on from our terrace.

I went off to town once a day to buy a chicken. A store in Moneglia sold whole roasted birds, and I'd head down about four to get today's and reserve tomorrow's. I'd supplement the chicken, which we'd pick on for a full day, with bread and olives from narrow, ochre-colored shops that lined Moneglia's pedestrian zone.

"Mom, there's a bag of stuff hanging on the door," said Adam one day as he left to play ping pong. I investigated and retrieved a plastic sack filled nearly to bursting with fresh apricots.

Nearly every afternoon for the rest of our stay we'd find a bag of apricots dangling from the doorknob. "More apricots!" Adam would shriek as he laid the newest delivery on the kitchen table. The kids loved them straight up and on the run. Mike and I assimilated them into our languorous sea-viewing sessions, pairing them with our landlady's young, label-less Vermentino. Ah, Moneglia. Glorious view; happy children; open spigot of almost-free wine; tasty chickens cooked by somebody else; juicy fruit delivered by anonymous produce fairies.

I decided the Germans were the apricot gifters. They had no terrace and no view, so no reason to hang around their apartment. Each morning about ten, they'd set off to hike, sporting backpacks, boots, and serious socks. We, in bathing suits, would look up from our terrace onto the mountainside planted with orchards and vines and see the family ambling amidst the agriculture. I figured they'd befriended a landowner who let them pluck his apricots, and they were using the fruit to pay Adam and Dana back for playing so much ping pong with their daughter.

Near the end of our stay I saw the German father in the parking lot, and I thanked him for the fruit: "Danke sehr fur die Aprikosen." He shook his head: "Nein, nein! Nicht von uns. Von der Schwester!"

Signorina Marina, the "sister," had delivered the apricots. We learned she owned not only the vineyards that produced our free flowing Vermentino, but all the groves and orchards we'd been looking on. She owned the mountainside. And she enjoyed sharing sips and pieces of it with her guests.

Lori Hein

Nurtured by Nature

The ideal growing conditions for grapes are a cold winter, a warm, wet spring, and a long summer with lots of sunshine during the day and cooler temperatures at night.

Grapes can grow in less ideal climates, as long as they benefit from reflected sunlight either from light-colored soils or bodies of water.

A light wind keeps the grapes from overheating and drying out, but too much wind can damage the vine or stunt its growth.

Too much direct, hot sunlight will cause the grapes to ripen prematurely.

However, when the ideal conditions are not present, grapes can benefit from a certain amount of stress. A vine that is forced to dig its roots deeper due to brief periods of drought or depleted soil can produce a small crop of very intense berries.

2

TICKLING THE TASTEBUDS

chanson du vin

I feel like a tiny bird with a big song!

Jerry Van Amerongen

We made our way carefully down the steep stairs of the small French château into the caves below the stone barn. The coolness was welcome after the hour spent strolling through gardens and gnarled grapevines under the merciless July sun with six others on our tour. Bright light bulbs hung down from the ceiling every ten feet, revealing decades of mold and dirt encrusting the walls. Huge oak casks lined large, barrel-vaulted rooms as far as we could see.

"Antoine, we are here!" called Jean Claude, our guide. He pursed his lips and squinted into the darkness. "Antoine, we're here for the tasting!"

"Ah, bien. Here I am!" A middle-aged man with a brushy mustache grumbled his way toward us out of the gloom.

"Bonjour, Jean Claude!" He smiled at us and gestured toward a wooden doorway to our right, "This way, please."

We followed him across the room, footsteps echoing as we filed into the square room with a heavy wooden table in the center. Eight bottles of wine stood by a large platter with cheese and thin slices of baguette. Black and white photographs of the château and the vineyard covered the walls. Antoine closed the door gently behind us, explaining that he didn't want to disturb the wine with all our noise. "Wine is alive," he told us. "It is sensitive to its environment."

Jean Claude filled eight glasses with red wine, which we sipped carefully as Antoine described the style of the wine, the quality of the vintage, and the rich history of the château. During World War II, the German general responsible for this region had taken exceptional care of all of the châteaux because he loved wine and knew the area well from childhood visits to relatives.

The tallest of the four men in our tour group cleared his throat. "We are members of a German singing group that performs at festivals all over the world," he said. An older, reed-thin man with him swished wine in his mouth and swallowed. "The sound here is so wonderful, it makes me want to sing to the wine." The others nodded.

We sipped wine and ate bread and cheese as Jean Claude opened more bottles from a wooden case under the trestle table. The delicious cheese was made by Antoine's brother, who left the family wine business at eighteen when he fell in love with a girl whose family owned a dairy. "Me, I like wine. I like growing the grapes, I like making the wine," Antoine explained. "Now my son is helping me. He'll be in charge one day, one day when I'm too old to get down the ladder!" He laughed.

One of our German friends started to hum, quickly joined by another. A third started to sing quietly, and then all four joined in together, their voices full, rich, and strong. Echoing in the small room, their song was exultant. They swung right into another when the first finished, singing different parts, calls, and responses. I didn't understand a word, but the emotion transcended any language barrier.

Antoine sliced more cheese, and we drank to the history of this little château as Jean Claude poured himself a glass and tore bread off a fresh baguette. Between songs, the singers, a little red in the face, drank reverently.

"And now, now, I must sing to the wine!" insisted one singer. He flung open the door and started a new song. The others joined him, their voices echoing far into the dim reaches of the caves.

🍷 *A Pairing to Try*

Cerdon du Bugey is a sparkling wine from southeastern France that tastes like a strawberry Creamsicle. A delicious aperitif or dessert wine that goes well with chocolate.

Antoine passed around chunks of a chocolate bar he pulled out of another wooden case.

Three songs later, Jean Claude looked at his watch, startled, and hit himself on the forehead. "Ah, we will be late for lunch. So sorry, Antoine, we must go. Right now!" He bowed to Antoine. "Merci, merci beaucoup!"

We obediently filed back up the stairs into the hot sun. As our eyes adjusted to the daylight, our group was quiet. My thoughts drifted. What history this small patch of French earth has witnessed, and what treasures lie just below us in quiet caves waiting for another song to be sung.

Louise Foerster

Identity Crisis

The French use a strict system to identify wines known as the Appellation D'Origine Contrôlée (AOC). Among other things, the French AOC identifies the grape varieties that may be grown in a geographic area, the maximum production per acre, and the minimum level of alcohol required for wines produced in the area.

The more lax American system is known as the American Viticultural Areas (AVA). An AVA is defined strictly by a geographic area. The only requirement for wine with an AVA designation on the label is that 85 percent of the grapes must be grown in that viticultural area. An AVA designation for a region is based on characteristics such as an area's topography, soil type, climate, elevation, and, to some extent, historical precedent. AVAs range in size from several hundred acres to several million; some reside within other larger AVAs. For example, California's Napa Valley is an AVA. The first AVA in the United States was the Augusta AVA in Missouri, established in 1980.

Thirty states have Federally designated AVA wine regions; Arizona, Arkansas, California, Colorado, Connecticut, Idaho, Indiana, Kentucky, Maryland, Massachusetts, Michigan, Minnesota, Mississippi, Missouri, New Jersey, New Mexico, New York, North Carolina, Ohio, Oklahoma, Oregon, Pennsylvania, Rhode Island, Tennessee, Texas, Virginia, Washington, West Virginia, and Wisconsin.

Whether designated an AVA or not, wineries exist in every state. Grapes are shipped in from growing regions, or wine is made from other fruits and plants including dandelion wine, apple wine, strawberry wine, even pineapple wine made in a winery in Hawaii.

A Taste of New Wine

When you travel, remember that a foreign
country is not designed to make you comfortable. It is designed to make its own
people comfortable.

Clifton Fadiman

I n the late summer of 1975, when my husband's
military assignment sent us to Lajes Field, Terceira
Island, our family arrived on one of the most historic and enchanting islands of the Azores Archipelago.

As we made friends, we kept being asked, "Have you
been to the vineyards to see the harvesting of grapes?"
This question evoked our curiosity. As we drove along the
cobblestone road, we saw ships sailing toward the port in
Praia da Vitória. We enjoyed the island's captivating old-
world charm. Pink and blue hydrangea flowers covering
four- to six-foot-high volcanic rock walls presented a magnificent vista. Wild flowers provided a garden bouquet of
a variety of colors and types in the rich volcanic soil. This
soil also produced an abundance of vineyards in the
foothills.

After a brief stop for our picnic lunch, I observed that
we were getting close to Biscoitos, our first destination on

the vineyard tour. Moments later, the silence was broken by our son Patrick, "Look! There are some men working in the vineyard close to that building!"

"I'm tired of riding. Are we going to stop here?" asked his sister Kristy.

"Yes, but remember, we must be polite and not do anything that would offend anyone," I cautioned.

Jim parked in the driveway of the winery. Quickly, he retrieved the Portuguese phrase booklet from the glove compartment, anxious to greet the men smiling and waving for us to get out of the car.

"Bon tarde. Como esta?" (Good afternoon. How are you?) We greeted them with smiles and enthusiasm.

The winery was built from unfinished stones and concrete, whitewashed and trimmed in reddish-brown. This was the standard way homes and buildings were constructed, except for size and brightly colored trim.

♟ A Pairing to Try

Vinho Verde is a white wine from Portugal. Vinho Verde is highly acidic and a bit bubbly with a low alcohol content, which makes it perfect for an afternoon picnic.

Inside was a large bare-walled room with a wine press. The floors were made from packed, dark, reddish-brown dirt. The adjoining room was smaller and held a rustic homemade wooden table on which I noticed a gray metal dishpan half-full of dirty water. Next to it were six or seven clear plastic glasses with small varying amounts of freshly-pressed new wine in them, and a filthy dish towel. I noticed the looks on the faces of my family and knew they saw my own uncertainty.

The Portuguese men asked us if we would like to taste the new wine, pointing toward the dirty glasses, then mimicking drinking with their hands. I was horrified, but the words, *We can't do anything to offend anyone*, kept reverberating in my head. I looked at the men with dirty, wine-stained hands, clothes and boots from handling and tramping down the grapes in the winepress. The men were so gracious and eager to share with us, how could we possibly chance insulting them by saying no, or by leaving.

Hesitantly, we smiled and nodded our heads. As we watched the man pour out the new wine remaining in the glasses on the dirt floor, swish them in the dirty water and then dry them with the filthy towel, I continued to pray silently. From the expressions on our children's faces, I knew they couldn't believe we were actually going to drink from those glasses.

Nevertheless, we lifted the glasses to our lips. Surprisingly, it tasted good. Before we could speak, the glasses were immediately refilled. We looked hopelessly at one another.

The men wanted to know how we liked it. With weak smiles, we replied, "Muito bane. Obrigado." (Very good. Thank you.) We knew they expected us to drink what they had given to us. I prayed silently for God to guide us and to protect our health. Instantly, helpful thoughts came to my mind. I remembered the varying amounts of new wine left in the glasses by the previous users. As Jim was trying to communicate with the men, I whispered to Patrick and Kristy, "Leave some in your glass and put your hand over the top." This worked for us when they offered to fill them up once more. Again, we told them, "No, obrigado. It was muito bane."

However, when Jim finished his second glass, they immediately refilled it! He gave me a questioning look, *What did you do?* I revealed my hand over the top of my glass of remaining new wine. He followed my example and it worked.

As we stepped outside, it was apparent that the winemakers wanted to show us something else. We noticed numerous large wicker baskets filled with clusters of grapes. They handed us a cluster of smaller grapes and motioned for us to eat them. They laughed at our expressions, as we tasted the sour grapes. Next, they handed us another cluster of larger grapes which had a sweet taste. After a few minutes of charades, we finally understood that the sour grapes were used for making cooking wine, while the sweet grapes were for eating and making drinking wine.

We thanked our hosts before climbing into the car and heading for home. In spite of the conditions, none of us came down with any mysterious illnesses, and it was a wonderful adventure that we would remember forever.

Minnie Norton Browne

Nonno's Wine

L'acqua fa male, il vino fa cantare
(Water is harmful; wine makes one sing)!
Old Lombardian Saying

T he vines came from Arsago Seprio, Provencia Lombardy, Nord Italia, wrapped in wet handkerchiefs pressed against his chest—symbols of his hope. Nonno patted them when he, my grandmother, my uncle, and mother said goodbye to everything they knew tethered to relatives on the Genoa dock. Their people had put one end of a yarn ball in each hand, and as the Duc d'Orca steamed northwest to New York, they unwound woolen umbilici until the green membrane of the sea was streaked by the severed cords and pricked by tears.

It was July of 1914. The First World War began a week after they settled into their tiny Little Italy apartment on Mulberry Street where water froze in glasses that first winter, and Mamma and Zio Dino slept in steamer trunks. Nonno's vines rooted in pots, lived on the fire escape and waited while he did endless twelve-hour days on the New York docks. Nonna, because she was a college-educated fine artist, set her easel up in Central Park, garnering rich ladies to whom she taught her fine Italian and oil painting.

Nonno's symbols of hope were finally planted, and bore fruit on Indian Neck Avenue in Branford, Connecticut, the home Nonno built that fulfilled their dream for a better life.

"Your Nonno sat for days not moving," Nonna told me. "He watched the sun, the pattern of rain under an umbrella, before he finally divined the spot for his wine cellar. When he turned the first shovel of dirt, we all cheered and cried, we were so happy!"

"It's your Nonno's religion, and his church," Mamma had added with a wry chuckle. "He dug his wine cellar before we even had beds! We camped in tents until he started building your Nonna's house over his wine cellar!"

The dark, pungent-smelling cavernous hole—the holy vino sanctum sanctorum—was entered from the underbelly of their house. Turning right, and after a dozen steps, total gloom reached out and ate sight like the whale did Jonah. Moist stones protruded here and there like hunched, swelled-bellied gnomes ready to grab a child, which I was then. New, capacious oak barrels rested sideways all along its sides, sporting barely-glinting metal spigots.

Outside, for twenty-five years, the original vines kept company with new varietal brothers and sisters, and twisted into great gnarled arms, birthing great bitter-seeded russet and purple orbs, which Nonno let spill down through his sausage fingers like Nonna's hair. Gatherers of morning frost, sun swindlers, mineral poachers, and air grabbers—his teeth would sever one, suck it, read the wine news, and finally grind the seeds in a sound I hear to this day. In the late summer, when Enrico Santo

DeBernardi's ken pronounced them ready, friends and family jumped into action.

At the first gathering, Nonno turned dark, oily wheels that moved round, wooden plates down upon the over-flowing baskets of grapes. The juice flowed like a maroon river from bottom spigots into a giant tub, smashing skins, seeds and stems from several varieties. With sugar content corrected, and wine acid added by his intuition, it would begin the barrel-aging process. Vino Rosso or Vino Bianco de Enrico Santo De Bernardi was beginning its ancient journey. Nonno would take long, sustained sniffs, narrow his eyes to slits, then nod his head this way and that, reading from one of the greatest, most ancient books of the world that wound back more than 10,000 years.

Our final result would be a big, thick red, with hints of oak and black cherry. Others were lighter, tasting of earth and stone. The delicate Vino Bianco, made from tiny champagne grapes in which only the juice was used, was Nonna's favorite. Effervescent, crystal clear and clean, in the style of the Piemonte sparkling, champagne-like dry varieties, it was kept in barrels longer and canted after two years. The more humble white was drunk quickly, or used in making veal scallopine for Sunday supper, or given to "dozayankisses," our family word for "those Yankees" who lived on the other side of Indian Neck Avenue.

"Ah, Puch," Nonno remarked on that summer day, using his pet name for me. "I bring these vines from Italy—Nebbiolo. It means 'mist.' The mist comes down from the Alps. The Romans planted it in my province, Lombardy, over 2,000 years ago! Now, you taste, and tell

🍷 *A Pairing to Try*

Aglianico, a varietal from Campania, Italy, goes well with pasta served with poultry or meat-based sauces. The vecchio and riserva wines also go well with second course dishes, either red meats or games.

your Nonno the vino veritas! The wine's truth!"

I sniffed the stained jelly glass, took some, and let it bathe the inside of my mouth. My ears itched. I closed my eyes.

"Buono. Virtuoso," I ventured, using some word grabbed from the great yonder of adult Italian.

"Your Nonna teach you that?" he asked, laughing heartily, pinching my cheek. His eyes told me I'd said the perfect thing. "Virtuous, eh?"

Many years have come and gone since those days. Recently on a trip east, I returned to my childhood home. Over eighty years old now, the fine foundations of the home still supported the wine cellar. The vines from Italy had long since gone wild, creeping here and there, over and into the flower gardens that once bloomed with such beauty. I closed my eyes and saw them all, in the full prime of their lives—those who'd cast such huge wine-colored shadows into which I'll dance forever.

On the soft summer evenings of my Albuquerque home, I raise a glass of vino rosso to Nonna and Nonno, to Mamma, and to them all, grown from my deepest roots, twined straight through my heart, fruit of memory, the wine of my soul. Bravo, la famiglia. Te amo, siempre.

Isabel Bearman Bucher

The Soup

The wine urges me on, the
bewitching wine, which sets even a wise
man to singing and to laughing gently, and
rouses him up to dance and brings forth
words which were better unspoken.

Homer

My soup cookbook is organized by months to take advantage of seasonal produce. "March" features French Onion Soup, which I order at restaurants but had never made. An approaching dinner party inspired me to try.

Many of our friends are gourmet cooks; I am not. I often pick their brains for ideas on how to perk up the ordinary. One said the secret for "best-ever" onion soup is to caramelize the onions before adding stock. Another said her secret was to use home made vegetable stock, "to accommodate vegetarians." Still another had two hints: use a variety of onions and add wine before serving. That last one sounded like a great way to fancy-up my dinner. Ultimately, I used all the tips.

Early on party day, I made my stock. The recipe called for eighteen cups of water; "add more if necessary." It was.

I used carrots, turnips, leek, onion, zucchini, celery, cabbage leaves, bay leaves, orange peel, parsley and black peppercorns. What a healthy first course this would be! After boiling it for a half hour, I savored the aroma as the stock simmered for the required two hours.

Carefully following the recipe, I strained the broth, reserving six cups for my soup. Having raised five children on a teacher's salary, I couldn't bear to discard the vegetables. I pureed them, returned them to the extra broth and froze it in quart jars.

Next, I thinly sliced six large onions: two yellow, two Bermuda, and two white. Not sure how large "large" is, I had selected onions the size of grapefruit. They mounded eight inches high in my spaghetti pot. As they browned in olive oil, I added sugar. My friend hadn't told me how much, so I added a half cup at a time. Perhaps this wouldn't be as healthy as I originally thought.

While stirring, I sampled our wine. It was strong. I set it aside to cant.

Soon, the onions glistened. I celebrated my success with another sip or two of the Merlot, which seemed smoother. Its sweet bouquet mingled with the scent of onions. Ah, clearly I was onto something.

Savoring the gourmet aroma of my kitchen, I added the six cups of vegetable broth. It seemed scant under all those onions. I already froze the extra broth. What to do? The wine bottle was handy. I added enough to cover all the onions. What a rich, grape color it was!

Amid the heady steam from my simmering soup, I prepared the entrée. Guests were bringing salad, potatoes and dessert. All I had left to do was set a pretty table. I was a little nervous about trying a new recipe for guests. Another sip of Merlot relaxed me as I went to dress.

Not certain just when "before serving" is, I added a cup of merlot to the soup as the first guests arrived. We visited, and caught up on family developments over beverages and light hors d'oeuvres. Soon it was time for dinner.

It suddenly occurred to me that the alcohol in the wine might have evaporated during all that simmering. I added another cup immediately before I scooped the soup into ramekins, topped each with a slice of French bread and grated cheese, and set them under the broiler. Within minutes, the soup was ready and we savored each spoonful.

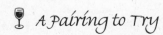 *A Pairing to Try*

Chimney Rock Elevage Stags Leap District 2003 Merlot, although not moderately priced, is a wine that can be enjoyed now through 2011. Merlots pair well with stews, hearty meats, and soups with a rich, vegetable base.

My efforts obviously bore fruit. Everyone raved about the soup. No one, however, remembers the entrée.

Diane C. Perrone

[Editor's Note: *Recipes for stock and soup are in* Twelve Months of Monastery Soups, *by Brother Victor-Antoine d'Avila-Latourrette, published by Triumph Books, Liguori, Missouri, 1996.*]

"I open a bottle of champagne every Friday.
Just getting through the week is
cause for celebrating!"

How (Not) to Open
a Bottle of Champagne

Energy and persistence conquer all things.

Benjamin Franklin

"Daddy, let me open the Champagne! Pleeeease?"

It was the last night of 1966, and I was twelve years old. My parents had agreed to let me stay up late for their New Year's Eve party, and I was almost as excited as I had been a week earlier on Christmas Eve. My younger sister and brother were in bed sound asleep, and I felt grown up and sophisticated—as much as a twelve-year-old can feel at a party for adults. I wore a new holiday dress that night and my very first pair of hose.

"Okay," Daddy agreed, looking like a bald Cary Grant in his new tuxedo. "Come over here by the sink, and I'll show you how to uncork a bottle of bubbly." He grinned as he untwisted the protective metal shield from the top of the bottle. "Here you go. Now, push up on the cork and it'll pop right out."

I worked at the cork with both thumbs, but it wouldn't budge. "I can't do it!"

"Sure you can," Daddy answered. "I'll get you started."

He pried the cork a quarter-inch upwards and then handed the bottle back to me. "Try again."

I gave my hero a cheerful smile, shook the magnum as I'd seen people do in the movies, and shot the cork directly into the fluorescent light above the sink. The resulting explosion sounded like a cherry bomb, and Champagne gushed from the bottle like a geyser, covering the kitchen floor and the front of my new dress. I squealed in horror as the broken fluorescent bulb showered the kitchen with tinkling glass and sent us running for cover into the living room.

Mama hurried from the dining room where she had been arranging a spread of delectable party food. "What in the world is going on?" she asked when she saw our shell-shocked expressions. "Have you two started the fireworks already?"

Daddy started laughing. He took the half-empty magnum of Champagne from my hands and gulped straight from the bottle. "Pretty good year, Mama," he said, offering the Champagne to her.

I looked down at my ruined party dress and felt like crying.

Mama must have known. "Oh, honey, it's okay," she said. "Let's get you washed up while Daddy cleans the kitchen." Mama swigged some Champagne and handed the bottle back to Daddy. "Come on," she said, taking my hand and leading me down the hall.

I changed into another dress, hoping the new one wasn't permanently ruined. Mama powdered my nose, and let me put on a little pink lipstick and a dab of White

Shoulders, saying that every woman should greet the New Year with as much glamour as possible. I was smiling again when the doorbell rang and I greeted our first guests.

"You're too young for Champagne, Sweetie, but how about a little ginger ale in a champagne glass?" Daddy said, once the party was in full swing.

🍷 *A Pairing to Try*

Moët et Chandon Brut Rose NV is a moderately priced Champagne and a delightful alternative to the traditional blanc Champagnes. It is an excellent aperitif, or delicious accompanying light poultry dishes and meat.

I nodded in agreement. I had sneaked a sip of Champagne earlier while my parents weren't looking and much preferred the taste of ginger ale. Mama put a glittery cardboard and crepe paper crown on my head and gave me a noise maker. But as might be expected, the grown-up party proved to be boring for a girl my age. I soon toddled off to my parents' bedroom to watch TV, taking my elegant glass of ginger ale and a full plate of party food with me. I fell asleep long before midnight.

Years passed before I managed to live down the debacle of shooting out the lights with a Champagne cork, but I made up for it by learning the proper way to handle sparkling wine. Now when I open a bottle of bubbly, I wrap a dish towel over the cork and push gently against it until I hear a slight pop. That's all there is to it.

And believe me, I much prefer the flavor of good Champagne or sparkling wine to ginger ale these days. Nor do I limit the joy of sparkling wine to holidays, birthdays, and anniversaries. Every day is a special occasion if you make it one.

Ruth Jones

Doña Felica's Vineyard

Our rural ancestors, with little blest
Patient of labour when the end was rest,
Indulged the day that housed their annual grain,
With feasts, and off'rings, and a thankful strain.

Alexander Pope

With its alternating patches of fields and muscatel vineyards, the Mancha region of Spain seems to stretch on forever. It's a land so flat that on nights of olden times you could see visitors approaching on horse, mule, or donkey who would arrive come daybreak.

A wavering curtain of hot air distorts the vision most of the day hours. As a kid, my summers were spent melting on the Mancha. My parents always took time to visit with family friend Doña Felica, a true noble, related to almost every royal lineage ever to rule Spain.

Her village transported us back to an earlier century. A Moorish tower dominated the estancia that Doña Felica referred to as her "modest country house," and it had enough rooms to keep a kid exploring an entire evening. What's more, old coaches were hidden in her old carriage house and musty stable.

Dusty crates and shelves were filled with clear and

green glass bottles bearing simple labels, not the least bit elegant. They'd only get filled if the grapes passed the harsh criteria of the grower. As far as the eye could see, Doña Felica's grapes basked in the sun of the Mancha. Traversing her fields, she seemed to know every plant by name. She identified two types of grapes, those that would make wine good enough to serve at her dinner table, and those meant be burned to industrial alcohol. She allowed no compromise.

A Pairing to Try

"Liquid bliss" is how *Wine & Spirits Buying Guide 2007* describes the Chambers Rosewood Vineyards Rutherglen Rare Muscat. On the expensive side, it is a dessert wine for that very special occasion. More affordable Rutherglen Rare Muscat's are no less satisfying.

I once saw the shocked face of a French wine trader who asked to buy some of the wine she considered the lesser quality. She informed him, in no uncertain terms, "that dishwashing water" would never leave her winery in a bottle, because she'd never allow it to go anywhere but the alcohol distillery.

I was fascinated by the gigantic clay vats for fermenting the wine, the oaken barrels to allow it to ripen, and the little basin I likened to a swimming pool, but in reality once served as the place grapes were stomped by foot.

Every summer, Doña Felica's youngest son, Mauricio, repeated his favorite joke. In the times when the grapes were still crushed with foot power, one of the neighbors produced a famed wine. Years later, customers started to complain about the reduced quality, and the neighbor confessed he couldn't find a wine stomper with the same sweaty feet as the one earlier.

Being a kid, I never sampled any of the wines she produced, but we got treated to all the grapes we could eat, and baskets more to take home. I thought I was in paradise.

Years later, whenever I sip a glass of Muscatel, I can't help wondering if Doña Felica would approve of the quality.

Alf B. Meier

Blame It on the Wine

One reason I don't drink is that I want to
know when I am having a good time.

Nancy Astor

I t happened on Halloween night in 1976, over thirty years ago. Why I'm sharing it now is no doubt due to the fact that I am still in need of redemption.

A year earlier, I'd divorced my husband and moved with my three young children back to Illinois where my parents still lived. The next year, I met Harold, the man who would eventually become my second husband.

On that fateful Halloween night, Harold drove down from Wisconsin to visit me. My brother Joe, a college student, was also in town visiting. After the children, ages four, five and seven, had finished their neighborhood trick-or-treating, my mother offered to babysit, so Harold, Joe, and I could go out on the town. Not one to turn down a chance for a few good laughs, I pulled out my tall, pointy, black witch's hat, black cape, long flowing dress, and a mask with the ugliest nose warts you've ever seen.

"I'll be the bad witch," I giggled in a creepy voice. "Harold, you be the good witch." I found an oversize, but fetching, floor-length, light-blue dress and a blond wig that I pulled on over my 6'3" boyfriend, much to his chagrin. A sparkly wand completed his look. My brother dressed up like some sort of weird-looking wizard.

We drove to town unsure of where we were actually headed. My brother was driving, and when he looked at Harold and me, he automatically turned into a liquor store.

Not being a connoisseur of wine, or anything else in the liquor department, I marched up to the counter and proclaimed in my best cackling witch's voice, "I'm thirsty, Mister, heh heh heh. Give me a bottle of wine that tastes like Kool-Aid. And make it snappy, Sonny. I've got a cauldron bubblin' and a few frogs to catch."

The young worker handed me a bottle of fruit-flavored Ripple. Harold and Joe bought a six-pack of beer to split.

I wasn't lying about being thirsty, and that bottle of wine went down real easy. It did taste a lot like strawberry Kool-Aid. At the time I wasn't a drinker of anything harder than iced tea or cocoa, and I was surprised at how good it tasted.

We hit a few local restaurants and stores downtown, prancing around like the good witch and the bad witch from the Wizard of Oz, with Merlin as our sidekick. I downed that big bottle of Ripple within the hour, getting louder by the minute.

The next thing I remember is waking up at home the next morning with all my clothes on. Harold came upstairs from the guestroom in the basement and informed me that we'd won first place in the dance contest at one of the most popular restaurants in town. I didn't even remember being in a dance contest, let alone winning first prize. Heck, I didn't even remember the restaurant.

I managed to crawl out of bed and sit on the living room sofa, ramrod straight, knowing full well that if my body touched anything it might self-implode. When the children started coming downstairs with their usual cheerful chatter, I motioned for Harold. In a whisper I said, "Take the children to church. Please don't let them talk before you leave. If anyone talks, my head will cave in or explode, I'm not sure which."

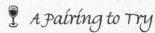

A Pairing to Try

Substitute sparkling wine for club soda the next time you're enjoying your favorite vodka. Sauvignon Blanc or Pinot Noir will add another layer of flavor to your cocktails. A perfect pairing for reception fare and finger-foods.

My future husband smiled, gave me two aspirin and a cool drink of water, and shuffled out the door with the children, leaving me to my miseries. If I remember correctly, that Ripple hangover lasted three full days. And it was nearly a dozen years before I could let a drop of bubbly touch my lips.

Since that day, I've never said the words "Ripple" or "Wine that tastes like Kool-Aid" to anyone who dispenses the fruit of the grape. I now know the difference between battery acid and good wine. Every so often, in an even-numbered year, when there's an eclipse, and someone is treating me to a fine meal in an elegant restaurant with another couple, I let them persuade me to order a bottle of good wine. I savor each sip. I make the bottle last through dinner. I don't order a second. And there's no after-dinner aperitif. I simply can't risk being in another dance contest.

Patricia Lorenz

A Glass of Bliss

Learning is not attained by chance,
it must be sought for with ardor
and attended to with diligence.

Abigail Adams

T he glass is raised to eye level. The deep, ruby liquid catches the light of a candle, creating instant romance in a glass. A deep breath brings a mélange of scents: fruit—strawberry perhaps, or raspberry. Definitely grapes, fresh and purple and sweet. Earthen tones. The barest hints of oak and spice.

Nature in hand.

Momentary heat on the tongue, rapidly replaced by the flavor of red as the alcohol fades away, leaving the true taste behind. Citrus wraps the tongue in berries, and pomegranate, and apple, and so much more.

How can all these flavors be contained in one mouthful of wine? That was what my wife and I wanted to find out for ourselves when we took our first wine vacation.

Ours is a story that is probably common around the country. When we first began drinking wine, we started with simple white Zinfandels. Neither of us enjoyed white wines, and while I could tolerate reds, their flavor was much too strong for my wife. The white Zinfandel was a perfect compromise; sweet and just a bit tangy, while at the same time, light.

As time went by, I grew bolder and began experimenting with reds. Nothing too robust; elegant Merlots, Zinfandels, and Pinot Noirs. At the same time, my wife and her friends veered into the territory of sweet and semi-sweet whites: Pinot Grigios, Rieslings, and some Chardonnays.

As we accumulated a list of labels we enjoyed, we decided to learn a little more about what was rapidly becoming a real hobby. We signed up for a wine weekend.

The event took place in Baltimore, Maryland, at the Admiral Fell Inn, a hotel that enjoys a reputation not only for classic, luxurious style, but also the presence of a ghost who has been known to wander the halls at night. It was into this romantic, Victorian setting that we arrived on a Thursday night, itinerary in hand. Our room was magnificent, with a bottle of wine and box of chocolates waiting for us.

Our weekend would consist of free breakfasts each morning. On Friday, we'd be treated to a wine and cheese party, where we'd sample local wines before dinner. On Saturday, we'd begin with a tour of a local winery, followed by a picnic lunch. Saturday night would be a formal wine-pairing dinner.

The Friday cocktail hour was excellent. The hotel's head chef doubled as sommelier and spent three hours taking us through a tasting of four whites, a rosé, and four reds. A brief history of each wine was provided, along with information on how to best pair the particular wines with specific foods. In between tastes we enjoyed a sampling of local fruits, vegetables, and a variety of cheeses.

🍷 *A Pairing to Try*

Martin Courtman, the Executive Chef of Sonoma Valley's Chateau Souverain, pairs Zinfandel with grilled or barbequed foods. He adds a Dry Creek Valley Zinfandel reduction to his signature barbecue sauce, and serves it with pork spare ribs and barbequed pork sandwiches.

Following the tasting, the hotel's manager allowed each of the six couples to choose two bottles of wine to take back with them.

"I don't see how this can get any better," my wife commented as we returned to our room.

"Well, tomorrow is supposed to be special. I hear we even get to keep the picnic basket," I replied.

The next day, our bus picked us up promptly at 11 AM for the half-hour ride to Boordy Vineyards. After a tour of the vineyards themselves, where we learned how soil and temperature affect the flavor of the grapes, we went through the wine-making process. It was here that I began to understand how and why certain wines have the flavors I enjoy or don't enjoy. Oak barrels, copper barrels, grape variety, even the location of the vineyards—all of it contributing to the complex mixture of flavors locked in the liquid.

I learned how to read the description of the wine, and know right away if it will be one that I'd enjoy. My personal preferences run to "hints of berry, cherries, pomegranate, and apple." If I see words like "spice," "oak," or "dry," I know I'll be better off avoiding that particular bottle.

The final event of the weekend was the wine-pairing dinner. It began with Champagne, strawberries (plain and chocolate-covered), and cheese and crackers. A woman from Boordy Vineyards presented a brief history of Champagnes and how they're manufactured. Then we moved onto dinner.

Over the course of the evening we tasted several whites and reds, along with a splendid dessert wine, and a port. Just as good was the conversation we shared with the other people at our table, most of whom were our age and just discovering a new level of wine appreciation as well.

We returned home full of knowledge, and with several bottles of new wines in our basket.

Today we make it a point of regularly going on wine tastings at local wineries and wine stores. Each time we go, we learn more and find new wines that we enjoy. It's also nice that when we go out to dinner with other couples, or with our parents, we are always asked to select the wine, and we can do it with ease.

Best of all, we can sit home and open a nice bottle of wine with dinner. Even if it's a simple meal on a busy night, raising a glass to each other never fails to capture that romance in a glass.

Greg Faherty

Muscat Cannelli

Blessed indeed is the man who hears
many gentle voices call him father!

Lydia M. Child

O n some especially dark days, I've wondered what I'd be willing to trade for just one more hug from my father. He died just as I was embarking on my own life, and there have been many milestones where I could have used his wisdom and comfort: career choices, marriage, divorce, custody battles, employment hassles. His wise optimism still lives as words in memory, of course, but the feeling of who he was seems to have faded over the years, emerging only in random flickers as brief as headlights across a bedroom wall.

"It's all there in your brain," my psychology professor told us, leaning over his podium. "Every minute you've lived. Everything you've read, felt, smelled. It's all there waiting for you to find it again." His gaze swept the room and his hands gripped dog-eared notes as he shared this amazing fact.

Maybe he was just trying to get better test grades from us, but I've never forgotten. Could the constituents of past reality—sight, sound, smell, and sensation—all be there, on file in my brain? What forgotten and unexpected treasures might I find? More importantly, could I recapture what it felt like to be near my dad again?

Before he could expound further on this, Dr. Fielding died and was replaced by a tall young woman who inexplicably wore galoshes to class and never mentioned the brain's power of memory. Again, death had shut a door. Yet, over a decade later I found myself reeling outside a winery tasting room reminded of what Dr. Fielding had said. I had opened it at last: the door to my past, so carefully secreted in the walnut-shaped amygdala, the brain's emotional memory broker, and what I found blew me away.

Standing in the Benziger tasting room, the cool darkness so welcome after Sonoma's hot dry air, I had tasted one wine after the other. They were all very good and each distinct. I considered how I might serve each. My father developed my nose for wine. He also loved to host dinner parties.

His job put him in an ideal position to invite the glitterati of the international medical world to our aging home on the outskirts of Washington, D.C. Weary of hotels and airplane food, these strangers would invariably come in the hopes of homey hospitality. They were never disappointed. My father could speak on any topic, in five languages, and had a repertoire of jokes that ran for a solid hour and a half. But before the entertainment, he wined and dined his guests with a gamut of carefully chosen wines, and I got to sample each one.

Sitting among the coifed and perfumed company in my shorts and bare feet, I would eat my dinner in silence, the better to observe their reactions to my father. As he made his rounds of the table, starting new glasses or refilling empty ones, he would comment on the wine he was pouring, speaking of its history and unique attributes. At the end I would receive maybe a finger's worth to try, and he would always ask me what I thought it smelled like. Total honesty was expected, so I soon learned that "like wood," "like mushrooms," "like cat" were not bad answers even if our guests laughed. Wine has a palette of flavors all its own.

But the wine I enjoyed drinking, rather than just experimenting with, was a particular Chenin Blanc. Sometimes, just to please me, my father would open it ahead of time so that I might have it with my supper. By the time dessert came, he'd shake his head slightly and give me only one finger's worth more, dark eyes twinkling. It was like liquid candy, and I never noticed that my tree-climbing abilities or monopoly strategy suffered. It was our special agreement: I could taste the wine but I could not get drunk.

My father always said that finding a wine you've enjoyed at a particular dinner is almost impossible after the fact because the environment and the food will not be the same. My attempts to locate this faintly green wine have turned into an exploration of the wines that pass by, but as he predicted, I have never found its equal.

As I tasted the last of a series of five wines in the Benziger tasting room, my wine room host could tell something was missing.

"Check this one out," he said, pulling a bottle out from somewhere along the counter. "It's our summer wine, and you can only get this one here." He rinsed out my glass and poured two fingers of a delicate, pale wine. He gave me a wise smile that seemed somehow familiar. "I think you'll like this."

One sip and I was barefoot again, the tops of my feet brushing against the starched linen table cloth. Sitting silent and upright at the table surrounded by illustrious company, I could sense my father seated at my right-hand side and smell his cologne. Then for an amazing, transforming moment, I felt again what it was like to have someone completely on my side. I felt his unconditional love for me. Where my struggles, and choices, and mistakes were all part of what made me lovable and important, and truly special to one other person. I nearly drowned in love.

🍷 *A Pairing to Try*

The Wine & Spirits Buying Guide 2007 gives the 2002 Savennières aux Moines Château from the Loire Valley in France a solid 94 rating. Florals of citrus and dried honey make this a perfect wine to accompany salads, mild to spicy rice dishes, sushi, seafood, and white meats.

Some people might stumble slightly when leaving a tasting room because the wines they've sampled have hit their brain just as bright wine-country sunshine hits their eyes. Upon leaving the tasting room's dreamy darkness, I stumbled too, but for a different reason: my brain, triggered by that delicious wine, redolent of summer and honeysuckle and apple, had given me an unexpected gift: the feeling of the love of a doting father for his only child. Dr. Fielding was right: it was still all there, just waiting for me to find it again in a sip of a simple, summer wine.

Valeria X. D'Alcantara

passing the cork

Necessity, who is
the mother of invention.

Plato

My husband, John, and I retired to Florida five years ago. While we enjoy an active lifestyle, we also spend quality time relaxing in our juxtaposed recliners, enjoying the stunning sunsets for which our state is famous, and sipping our favorite jug wine, Paisano. A good life indeed.

In an attempt to refine our taste in the fruit of the vine, our children have gifted us with bottles, books, and banter. Under their tutelage, we've enjoyed Dom Pérignon for milestone celebrations, and Grand Vin de Château Latour to welcome in the new millennium. We have an understanding of ameliorated, ripe, seamless tannins and the benefits of wine pairing. We now respect the simple cork, which is harvested from the bark of the Portuguese Cork Oak tree, and marvel at its ability to snap back after withstanding 14,000 pounds of pressure per cubic foot. It can mold itself to unusually shaped openings.

Son David called this spring, "Mumma, could you and Dad spend a couple weeks with Sophie? Marcie and I need a little aloha." Missing him and his wife, and their fluffy white pooch, we quickly obliged. John readied the car, and within a week we visited with them for a few days before their flight to the Big Island. Evenings found us in the stone and brick wine room, relaxing around their "tasting and toasting" table, warmed by the glow of the newly set sun filtering in through the stained glass windows. Laughter and lively conversation echoed throughout the house through the filigree, iron door.

On the first night of our visit, David selected a 2000 Clos Pegase Reserve Merlot, a velvety vintage, bursting with black cherry and spice, from the climate-controlled wine cabinet. I remembered my all-time-favorite toast, honoring Marcie in celebration of her being cancer free for five years. David ceremoniously popped the cork of a Schramsberg Crémant and lifted his glass to his beloved wife, graciously extolling her victory. His heartfelt sentiments touched us all deeply.

With our wine enjoyed and conversation finished, the men headed outside while Marcie and I prepared supper. When ready, we found them in the zen garden bent over the pedestal fountain engaged in an animated technical discussion. Something about stripped threads, sealing material and measurements for a replacement part that would likely have to be special-ordered. Seeing the object of their attention, I remembered a large bowl of signed corks in the pantry. Retrieving them and eyeballing a close match, I selected a cork from a 1997 Silver Oak estate-bottled Cabernet Sauvignon enjoyed by our family at a reunion several years ago. I touched each signature and hugged their collective essence to my heart for a brief moment. "That wine was the liquid manifestation of grape perfection," David reminisced, studying the cork. "Like butter," Marcie added. My sentiments exactly.

With a grand flourish, I inserted the cork into the hole. We each gave it a ceremonial good luck push. "Let the filling begin," I proclaimed. A perfect waterproof fit. A one-of-a-kind, cohesive monument to our family. With the cork signed, sealed and delivered—not necessarily in that order—we frolicked and two-stepped around the fountain.

John and I have since added a few special occasion bottles to our room temperature wine cabinet, and our taste in wine has become a bit more selective. We occasionally forgo beer with our pizza, pairing it instead with a Pinot Noir. Nevertheless, we are still in sync with inexpensive varietals. The savings help to soothe our taste buds, and the compound interest mellows the tannins' ragged edges. A few times a week, we relax in our juxtaposed recliners, enjoy the stunning Florida sunsets, raise our glasses in joie de vivre and toast our heirs—with Paisano.

Colette J. Sasina

A Pairing to Try

Kaesler's 2004 Grenache-Shiraz-Mourvedre Barossa Stonehorse is one of Australia's finest contributions from this free-spirited grape of the wine world. A roast chicken or burger bring out the inherent fruitiness of Grenache-based reds.

An Ounce of Prevention

Drink no longer water, but use
a little wine for thy stomach's sake
and thine often infirmities.

New Testament St. Paul, 1 Timothy, 5:23

As we raised our glasses high, Nonno's words sang out over the dining table, "Saluté per chinto anno," his deep, rich voice as hardy and pure as the red wine he held in his glass. "Good luck, for a hundred years," his dinner guests echoed back.

My grandfather's face beamed with pride at these joyous occasions, and our meal never began until each family member had repeated the traditional dinner toast and sipped from our small glasses of red wine. Wine was always a part of our family's holiday meal. And, like most Italian-American kids, I was introduced to its flavor, as well as its medicinal benefits, at an early age.

As each family milestone occurred—baptisms, first holy communions, confirmations, birthdays, graduations and marriages—another bottle of my grandpa's homemade red wine was uncorked. Bottles were poured on Sundays, holy days of obligation, and all national holidays; there was always cause for celebration in my grandfather's house. Grandpa believed that wine, in moderation, was a good thing, and my grandparents lived by the rule: "A glass a day keeps the doctor away."

My grandmother often put the benefits of red wine to good use as a medicinal cure. It was administered as a remedy for arthritis, and to purify the blood, cure anemia, alleviate stomach cramps, and prevent infection. During World War II, when cases of trench mouth and whooping cough reached epidemic levels in the United States, she administered the rich, red wine to each grandchild as a preventive mouthwash and gargle. Wine was also used as a remedy for cold sores or skin infections. Grandma poured a little wine into a saucer and let it stand covered overnight. In the morning, she dabbed the wine on the sore.

As a teenager, I recall the looks of astonishment on the faces of my non-Italian friends as they watched Papa fill my dinner glass with wine. To those who objected, Papa would simply say, "Wine is served in church at the communion rail, is it not? And it was served at the Last Supper." End of discussion. Papa's house was a peaceful one, and a place where he felt happiest. He had his own quiet corner, to which he retreated after a robust meal. It was his belief that the soul sighs after eating a large, traditional dinner, and that one should spend time in contemplation and reflection. Papa reflected at least an hour after every meal—the sound of his contented snore vibrated though the house.

October is my favorite time of the year, when the air is brisk, and leaves turn a vibrant rainbow of colors. Papa looked forward to this autumn month, too, but for a different reason. October is the traditional time of year for winemaking. It's the transition month between summer and fall, a time when papa gathered his paraphernalia and ingredients for the making of his hearty red wine.

Winemakers on the East Coast had to wait for good winemaking grapes like Malaga and Zinfandel to come in by rail car from California. But Santa Clara Valley winemakers, like Papa, were lucky enough to have the plentiful grapes of the Napa and Almaden valleys practically in their backyards. They only had to drive to local vineyards to buy boxes of the finest grapes.

Some old-timers nurtured their own tiny grape vineyards for the express purpose of making their own red wine. Devoted winemakers like Papa usually owned their own grape crushers, while others rented or borrowed one each fall. After the crush was finished, the juice was poured by funnel into the huge oak barrels, which had been cured with sulfur smoke. Here's where the talent for good winemaking would come in. One mistake and the winemaker's barrels would be filled with vinegar instead of wine. But, like Papa, most winemakers had inherited their skills from the Old Country and rarely made a bad batch.

Grandma's kitchen was the hub of activity preparing for

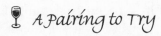 *A Pairing to Try*

Chianti is the life-blood of Italy. It's difficult to go wrong with a Chianti Classico Riserva or a Vino Nobile di Montepulciano. Even the inexpensive Chianti Rufina is a delight paired with pasta, pizza, or a piece of Parmigiana-Reggiano cheese.

a grand October feast, while the men in the family gathered in the cellar to cure the wine barrels and to help father set up his winepress. Some helped Papa haul in the grapes; others set up the grape crusher, while others cured the oak barrels. While we worked, Grandpa and Grandma would tell us stories of the renowned vineyards of Brolio Castle, the baronial estate of the Ricasoli family, an area famed for its Chianti wine. Wine has been made in this region of Italy since 1000 CE, and this revered standard of Chianti is what Papa tried his best to clone, its benefits passed down from generation to generation.

Only recently, thanks to modern medicine, do we now have proof that wine can aid digestion and wipe out bacteria better than bismuth salicylate (Pepto Bismol). Of course, all of this wouldn't be any news to Grandma Isolina and Grandpa Antonio, who lived well into their nineties enjoying a daily glass of papa's red wine.

Cookie Curci

The Beginning of a Beautiful Relationship

*Good friendships are fragile things
and require as much care as any other
fragile and precious thing.*

Randolph Bourne

Morocco: Trip of my dreams, born of a chance lunch, a leap of faith, and sustained by a medium-bodied, red wine produced in a Muslim country.

I was forty-one, a social worker at a mental health center on the North Side of Chicago. Barbara was fifteen years my senior and our office manager. We'd worked together six years, but hardly knew each other, and had never gone to lunch until a spring day in 2001.

"I need to decide whether to go back to Vienna for my timeshare period in the fall," Barbara said, fork in hand, when our discussion at the Thai restaurant turned to travel. "It's nice, but I'd also like to try someplace new."

"I have an airline voucher that's going to expire," I said, putting down my chopsticks. Suddenly, we were planning a trip together.

Barbara traveled extensively overseas, and I had done a

bit myself. As we pored over her timeshare property list-
ings, any country either of us had visited was out. Then,
there was the Hotel Ahlen Moghane, near Rabat,
Morocco's capital. A picture promised a room decorated in
deep red, its ceiling draped in sheer fabric. Magical. I had
dreamed of visiting Morocco since reading James
Michener's *The Drifters* at an impressionable age back in
South Dakota.

Our ambitious three-week journey would start in
Madrid, and include stops in Granada and the British territory of Gibraltar on the way to Morocco, before we
returned to Spain and Portugal. We took an introductory
Spanish course, and familiar with tapas and paella, we felt
somewhat prepared for Spain. But Morocco? We needed
to know more, and began our discovery at one of
Chicago's few restaurants featuring Moroccan cuisine,
L'Olive. We were surprised to see the short list of
Moroccan wines on the menu. Moroccan wines? Didn't
the Muslim culture prohibit alcohol?

"Morocco has a thriving wine industry," our waiter,
Ahmed, told us. He took the liberty of selecting a medium-
bodied red from the Les Celliers de Meknès vineyard, Les
Trois Domaines. Delightful! We toasted our upcoming trip,
Ahmed, and each other.

The trip did not start as smoothly as that night in the
restaurant. Our flight into Madrid was delayed. It took us
hours to find the hotel in Granada, and Gibraltar was
even worse. Problems developed prior to boarding the
ferry from Algeciras, Spain, to Tangiers, Morocco, but once
we finally landed, we felt confident we could make the

172-mile trip to the to Hotel Ahlen Moghane.

The two-lane road was in good condition, the pavement solid, but the road had no shoulder and was packed with vehicles, carts, people walking and riding donkeys and horses, and hundreds of goats. By the time the traffic finally eased, it was getting dark, and the road became curvy. Just outside the town of Asilah, we saw a billboard advertising the Hotel Al Khaima.

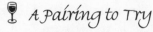 *A pairing to Try*

The Bekaa Valley in Lebanon is one of the world's original wine-producing regions. Chateau Musar continues to produce a very good red wine from a blend of Cabernet Sauvignon, Carignan, and Cinsault. Much like a Bordeaux, a better complement to lamb cannot be found.

"Maybe we should stop for the night," Barbara suggested.

"I just want to get to Hotel Ahlen Moghane!" I snapped. But less than a mile later, fatigue overtook me, and I turned the car around.

The brilliant, white stucco walls of the Hotel Al Khaima appeared as a mirage. Our room was simple, but clean and tidy. The balcony was open to the elements, with no doors or screens, and there was a gentle breeze off the shockingly blue Atlantic Ocean. We saw three men trekking across the beach, each with a camel in tow.

At the hotel's restaurant, Barbara did well enough ordering with the French she thought she had long ago forgotten. The menu included Moroccan wine, and we did our best to pick out the one we had tried at L'Olive.

"I didn't think we'd make it," Barbara said. "You did a terrific job driving."

"I'm sure your prayers helped," I said, laughing. "We make a great team."

Then the waiter returned with our bottle of wine. Sure enough, it was the same wine we'd tried at L'Olive. Finally, we were safe and relaxed, and had found something familiar and comforting in the journey—and in each other—where once there had been only the different and unfamiliar.

The trip continued to be a true adventure, with great challenges and moments of unspeakable wonder. Although we did not make it to the Meknes vineyard where our favorite Moroccan wine is made, we found a liquor store in Rabat and bought a few bottles to share along the way. The wine sustained us at every significant point the rest of the trip—most significantly in Seville, where I stopped to buy postcards and stamps at a little store. It was September 11, 2001.

Back at our hotel, the first on our excursion to have English language news, we were glued to BBC news coverage. That night, we shared a bottle of our precious wine in complete darkness, and near total silence. Our friendship was cemented that day. As we progressed through Portugal and back into Spain, visiting churches took on a new importance, as did sharing our wine.

"It's hard to believe we didn't know each other at all six months ago," I said, as we toasted the last night of the journey and finished the last bottle in Madrid.

"I didn't want to tell you this before, but I was really afraid to go to Morocco," Barbara confessed.

"I had no idea!"

"But it was such an amazing adventure. I wouldn't have missed it for the world and I would have never done it without you."

On our three-week trip through exotic and foreign lands, we traveled nearly 11,000 miles, drove over 2,300 miles, visited eighteen cities, slept in fourteen beds, rented three cars, took two ferries, became lifelong friends and shared one beloved wine.

Maureen Rigney

1863 Madeira

There is a communion of
more than our bodies when bread
is broken and wine drunk.

M. F. K. Fisher

G reat wines are determined by more than grape DNA alone. Making good wine requires sound principles and dedication to tradition. An impeccable bottle of wine is like a great family; they are priceless, rare, nurtured into existence, and against all odds, protected.

After four years of being a cancer patient, I couldn't claim a complete victory, but I was in the lead. I missed my brothers, so I traveled to Manhattan for a summer weekend of fun with Mark, Dean, and his wife, Maria. We planned to feast our way through the city, and vowed not to sleep. On our first night in the Big Apple, we dined on the terrace of a famed French restaurant that overlooked Central Park west.

"Should we do it?" Dean's eyes peered above the dessert wine list with a twinkle. There was no question. He was ordering the 1863 Madeira with dessert. My brother was a gastronome, with an insatiable passion to lavish on the ultimate indulgence.

"C'mon, we might never have this opportunity again. Besides, how often do we get a chance to be together? You can't put a price on this," he urged. He was the debater in the family. As an ex-Marine his views on most subjects were extreme and gave no room for liberal thinkers. This time, he was right.

Growing up a short distance from New York City, we weren't accustomed to dining on silver, fine porcelain, and crystal. We wore our share of hand-me-downs, and in the lean times of the 1980s learned to like the taste of government cheese. We eventually earned seven college degrees among us and had resumes to give any parent bragging rights. Driven to succeed, we found our adult lives gave little time for each other. But, there on the restaurant dining terrace, we laughed and talked about the future as we sipped forgettable late–20th century French red and white wines of excellent years.

"1863? It must be a fake," I chimed. With two more days in the city, I felt cautious about blowing it all on one extravagant bottle of vintage Madeira.

"You only live once," said Mark. His military unit had returned from the Middle East. It was a relief to be next to him instead of having the daily torture of not knowing if he'd be among the captured and beheaded. Occasionally, I'd receive a cryptic shipboard e-mail from him: "Am fine. Watch CNN and you'll know."

"Uh, did you big spenders see the price of that Madeira?" Maria spoke as she wiped mashed potatoes from her son's hair. In classic toddler fashion, my nephew had endeared himself to the patrons and staff. More than once, he scampered unnoticed to tug the pant legs of well-heeled gentlemen, and hems of posh, bejeweled ladies. If not for the waiters, he'd have earned the fastest time on record for a toddler sprinting down Fifth Avenue. Like a young wine, he too would mellow with age. Still taking his liquids from a sippee cup, though, he was uninterested in our adult quest for extraordinary grapeage.

"For that price I'll step on those grapes and make it myself," Maria said. An image of her squishing grapes between her toes made us explode with hyena laughter.

🍷 A Pairing to Try

Madeira wines from Portugal are like no other wines in the world. In the fortified wine category (alcohol has been added), they can be found in fine wine stores or ordered online. Bual, Malmsey, and Sercial are excellent values. Madeiras are a perfect complement to pork roasts, and when added to a mushroom gravy add a layer of flavor guests will not forget.

"Can I answer any questions for you sir?" A white-gloved waiter instantly appeared. He leaned towards Dean who still clutched the dessert wine list. Dean pointed, "This 1863 Madeira, can I see it please?"

"Yes, of course, sir."

With the waiter out of sight, Maria whispered, "Do you know how many weeks of groceries I can buy for this one bottle? Heck, my father can make this for nothing."

"He can't make an 1863 Madeira from Portugal," Dean retorted. Mark and I listened as they bantered. Established vineyards on her dad's upstate New York farm produced wine like their Italian ancestors did. For them, *la familia* meant everything. They were a passionate family, unafraid to show their affection. Nothing could diminish their loyalty to tradition, or to each other, not even an ocean. As much as I adored my sister-in-law, for this reason I envied her, too.

A year earlier, I urgently needed a bone marrow transplant but could not find a perfect bone marrow donor. I had already received months of chemo and radiation and had a failed bone marrow transplant using my own stem cells. In a race against time, doctors began a desperate global search of marrow registries. Months passed, and no donor matches were found, not even among my brothers. I hoped that whether by God, science, or evolution, a DNA match existed for me and would be found in time. More time passed, my cancer grew, and soon a secret was revealed. We had a sister.

Like a rare, priceless wine, a biologic sister represented more than a million-to-one shot at finding a marrow match. She was a missing piece of our family history and for me, also represented a twenty-five percent chance of my ultimate survival and freedom from cancer. Only my mother had the legal authority to search for her, and for months she flatly refused saying, "My hands are tied." At times she denied having another daughter. At other times she'd say, "I can't help you. What will everyone think of me if they knew the truth?"

The very idea that a shameful, decades-old family secret might be revealed rattled my mother, and the few remaining elders in our family who knew, to the core. A moral dilemma ensued between them about whether to search for my sister and save my life. As a result, a family cesspool uncorked a legacy of blame, deceit, and betrayal more suited for the imaginations of soap opera writers. A great flood of truth unearthed many more skeletons. I felt abandoned. My confidence, purpose, and value as a human being was shaken, and again mercilessly assaulted by a harsher knowledge. That fall, a court judge unsealed dusty adoption records to reveal my sister's identity. She was not a marrow match.

A year later, I sat on the terrace of a Manhattan restaurant, heard the clip-clop sound of horse-drawn carriages, and though emotionally scarred, I was alive. Our waiter returned with the Madeira. Surely, my credit card would get the biggest shock of its little plastic life. I felt a twinge of guilt and exhilaration.

"Wow, it's real after all," I said. "Let's go for it!"

We paused to marvel at how one bottle had survived wars, a transcontinental voyage, and human temptation. It had never been neglected by the hands that touched it, and now it was on our table. We raised our glasses.

"Tonight, we're drinking history," said Dean. "Here's to us and to this moment."

The Madeira tasted every bit of perfection. Like art, its burgundy color swirled beautifully in my glass. I breathed deeply and felt a tingling sensation run through my veins. I glanced at my nephew, so innocent, so loved.

I couldn't change the past. I wouldn't forget it either. The future was unknown. So, I went forward.

Milan Moyer

Peachy Keen

Wine is proof that God loves us
and wants us to be happy.

Benjamin Franklin

"Thanks for babysitting." I puffed a breath at the bangs plastering my forehead, damp from exertion and the mid-July heat wave.

"What did the doctor say?" my neighbor asked.

"He told me I need sleep, and he can't prescribe anything this late in the pregnancy and . . . he suggested wine." I rolled my eyes at the absurdity. "Can't you just see me bellying up to the bar and requesting something that would knock me out?"

With a hearty laugh Joyce patted my two-weeks-overdue girth. "Well, maybe you *should*."

"I wouldn't even know what to ask for." I shrugged. We both knew I had never imbibed. Grabbing my three-year-old with one hand, and my toddler with the other, I waddled to our house at the end of the cul de sac. Mere minutes later, the doorbell rang.

"Here. This'll do the trick." Joyce pressed a brown sack in my hands. "It's fruity. You'll like it."

"Wine? But . . ."

"Doctor's orders," she insisted, before she turned and fled.

With some hesitancy—and much curiosity—I placed the gift on the kitchen counter and pulled out the partially empty bottle. It *did* smell fruity, like peaches, perhaps. I set it aside and, squaring my shoulders, faced the long evening ahead. With my husband working late that night, dinner and bedtime weighed heavily on my sagging shoulders.

After the kids were fed, bathed, pajamaed, story-booked, lullabied, and tucked, I collapsed in a hot, weary heap on the couch, too tired to care that I hadn't eaten any supper.

What I wouldn't give to have air conditioning . . . and one night of sound sleep, I thought. *Just one.*

In a sudden decision, I padded to the kitchen and uncorked the bottle. Reaching into the cupboard, I grabbed a slender juice glass. Tupperware. Pastel pink. An omen, I hoped, for having a girl. But, how much would it take to make me sleepy? I poured the glass halfway. Realizing it was an awfully skinny glass, I added a bit more.

"May as well fill it to the top," I muttered.

I experimented with a sample sip and sputtered. It certainly smelled better than it tasted. So, pinching my nose to ease the onslaught of my senses, I tossed the entire contents to the back of my throat and choked it down in one foul swoop. Then I hid the evi . . . put the bottle in the back of the pantry. Norm would be home within the hour; I settled on the couch to watch a favorite show.

"Yum. Have you been baking pies?" my husband startled me awake.

Pies? In this heat? I giggled at the outlandish idea.

"How was your day?"

My day? I giggled because the question sounded funny.

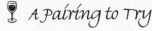

A Pairing to Try

A good Riesling has fruit florals and refreshing acidity which pair well with smoked fish, Indian curries, and baked ham.

"You ready to hit the sack?"

I giggled louder and longer, and I didn't even know why.

That night I got the sleep the doctor had hoped for. A lovely, sound, comfortable, dreamless sleep . . . until even, rapid—hard—contractions tugged me awake.

"Honey, it's time." I elbowed Norm. "We need to get to the hospital."

He flew into action. He knew the routine. Dress. Call the neighbor to babysit. Grab the suitcase.

I hesitated at the front door. "Go on and back the car out of the garage. I forgot something."

In a wink, I'd lumbered to the kitchen, filled another tumbler with the fruity quaff, and tossed it to the back of my throat. This time, it slid down easier.

At the hospital, my doctor leaned over the bed and patted me on the wrist. "With your history of hard labors, I sure hope you got a bit of sleep tonight."

Only a bit of sleep? I giggled at the outlandish idea. He sniffed and leaned in a bit closer. "It appears you took my advice."

His advice? I giggled because he sounded funny.

"Well, let's check you out."

I giggled even louder and longer, and I didn't care why.

Easiest labor I'd ever had. A girl. A peach of a baby girl.

Carol McAdoo Rehme

The Evolution of an
Amateur Vintner

With years a richer life begins,
  The spirit mellows:
Ripe age gives tone to violins,
  Wine, and good fellows.

John Townsend Trowbridge

When my father suggested that he and I try brewing our own wine, I was admittedly leery. My only experience in viniculture was a vague recollection of an elaborate set up in the basement of our family home many years ago.

It was the early sixties when my mother and her sister decided to try their hand at making wine. (I should point out that the antics of these particular sisters are legendary within our family.) The extent of their research on the art of winemaking amounted to watching an episode of *I Love Lucy* in which Lucy and Ethel stomped the fruit-of-the-vine in hilarious fashion.

They scoured local second-hand shops and rustled up the equipment needed to start their operation: a couple of shell-cracked, twenty-five-gallon crocks and several miles of siphon hose. They ordered what seemed like a ton of luscious, deep purple grapes and set to the messy task of juicing them.

I can vividly recall the sensation of the cool, meaty fruit oozing between my freshly scrubbed seven-year-old toes, and the sticky squirt of juice on my legs as I marched on-the-spot in a twenty-five-gallon crock. My toenails were dyed a nifty shade of black by the process, and the skin on my feet was tinted blue for several days afterward.

I have no idea what happened to the contents of the crock after it left the kitchen, or what rituals took place in the dim light behind the furnace, but we all grew familiar with the heady fragrance of fermenting fruit wafting from the basement. Successful vintages were celebrated with wonderful toasts—the disasters, however, were silently flushed down the toilet, and on one occasion, wiped off the walls.

I remember waking one night to the sound of breaking glass and popping corks. Apparently a temperamental batch of banana wine had blown its top and the bottles were exploding under the basement stairs. I believe this marked the end of my mother's winemaking adventures.

Fortunately, the art of amateur winemaking has evolved over the years. It is now a consumer-friendly enterprise attractive to even the apprehensive vintner. When my Dad and I ventured into our local "You-Brew-It" a few years back, we were armed with little more than an appreciation of red wine and the desire to brew our own for Christmas. Our experience was so rewarding that we have been making our own wine ever since.

We have our system down to a science; every six weeks or so we saunter in, bottle two batches of wine, and set two new ones to perk. Our greatest challenge has been choosing the type we want to make—the selection is overwhelming—Barbera to Zinfandel.

We take turns being the starter of the new wine, a process which encompasses sprinkling a package of yeast over a giant bucket of juice (it's exhausting but someone has to do it). Six weeks later, we return with our stash of wine bottles, an impressive and varied collection of glass finery, gathered from the recycling bins of family and friends. I am the designated filler of the bottles, and my dad is the corker—we work like a finely-tuned machine. Winemaking is serious business. The entire process takes just under an hour. We never get our feet dirty, the house never smells, and we end up with sixty bottles of wine—does life get any better than that?

Elva Stoelers

🍷 A Pairing to Try

Sake is a sulfite-free wine made from natural ingredients. Japan's Nanbu Bijin Southern Beauty is brewed with water that is naturally purified through mountain rocks. An ultra-premium grade, it is made from Ginginga rice of which at least 40 percent of the grain is polished away. An elegant, soft fragrance, and a flavor that shows pear and Muscat grapes, it can be served at room temperature, warmed, or chilled. Pair with Asian-inspired dishes, most fish, and poultry.

All the Comforts of Home

Excellent wine generates enthusiasm.
And whatever you do with
enthusiasm is generally successful.

Philippe de Rothschild

M y ideal wine pairing? A nice red accompanied by dehydrated Thai noodles and thimbleberries. Can't forget the thimbleberries. Or the Lake Superior view. But I get ahead of myself. Let me back up. Literally. Let me just unload the forty-five pounds I've been lugging around this island onto the picnic table—ahh—and start from the beginning.

Backpacking is my husband's passion.

Now, I like being outside. Really, I do. For five summers, my job was riding my bicycle as a tour leader for an outdoor vacation company. I've competed in a (mini) triathlon. I've even camped before. But give me Mother Nature in four- to six-hour doses. At the end of the day, I like two things: a hot shower and a bed.

So the idea of a multi-day, twenty-mile hike, with shelter and sustenance borne on our backs, felt more foreboding than fun. That our destination was Isle Royale, a remote island requiring a six-hour boat ride through notoriously rough Lake Superior waters, added another layer of trepidation. Isle Royale is the least-visited national park in the whole country. *There must be a reason,* I thought —after our visit, I knew why.

But I kept my doubts private as Mike meticulously planned our route and trip. Watching him pour dehydrated something-or-other into a zip top baggie, it occurred to me one way the trip could be mitigated.

"How about we bring a bottle of wine?" I suggested.

"Wine?" Mike said. "We can't bring wine. The bottle's too heavy."

"We could pour it into something else," I persisted. "One of these." I picked up a Nalgene, plastic bottles which are to backpackers what diapers are to babies.

Mike's face was dubious. He was already exceeding his preferred weight load with a menu designed for taste (my priority) rather than optimal caloric thresholds (his). "I don't know. They probably don't allow alcohol in the park."

"Oh, come on." I dismissed law enforcement concerns with a wave of my hand. "Who's going to know?"

And so, it turned out we landed on Isle Royale late on a late-summer evening, packs laden with sleeping bags, sleeping pads, extra socks, a first-aid kit, lots of dehydrated edibles, and numerous Nalgenes, including one filled to the top with Merlot. Nothing fancy—straight off the grocery shelf.

Twilight was deepening to dark as we stepped off the National Park Service ferry. Rough waters had postponed our departure from Michigan's Upper Peninsula, so we were arriving several hours later than expected. Mike was anxious to get going, lest we fall further behind schedule on our five-day hike.

"Got your headlamp on? Okay, let's go," he said, shouldering his heavier-by-far pack and setting off on the trail that paralleled the island shore, where cold waves lapped.

My walking stick clunked irregularly against the rock as I followed. Like the lake, my doubts were churning, again. Was I really up for spending the little vacation time we had on a no-frills—no running water, even—trip like this? This was no woodchip nature trail. This was real backcountry, complete with wolves and moose and water that required filtration. And now it was really dark.

We covered the three miles more quickly than I'd expected, however. Guided

🍷 A Pairing to Try

One of the best buys in wine are Chilean. Chile produces a high-quality wine at low prices due to low land and labor costs. Try the delicious Sauvignon Blanc, Cabernet Sauvignon, and Merlot. The Carmen Chardonnay Reserve 02 pairs well with smoked ham, pork chops, lobster, grilled salmon, or striped bass.

by the glow of our headlamps, we even found a site with a lake view. Mike lit his tiny camp stove for our almost-midnight supper, a Thai-flavored dehydrated something-or-other.

Surrounded by fifty-degree water, it was much colder here than the mainland. I put on my fleece pullover and sat at the picnic table, watching. I realized that Mike had planned this painstakingly. We had been married just over a year, and planning usually fell to me. *It was nice to have him take over*, I thought, clicking off my headlamp to better see the brilliant stars. Cozy in my pullover, and the security of togetherness, backpacking started to seem okay after all.

Uncorking the wine Nalgene, our plastic cups clunked as we toasted. The tangy peanut sauce and the dry red made a fabulous flavor combination. Dessert was a handful of thimbleberries, a tart, delicious relative of the raspberry that flourishes in the Upper Peninsula, plucked right off the bushes surrounding our site. Sated and exhausted, we crawled into our tent.

Well, to make a long story short, it turned out the only word to describe that trip is *perfect*. Perfect weather—days sunny but not hot, cool evenings just made for a down sleeping bag. Perfect companionship—whether we were hiking, hanging around the campsite, or making a midnight pit stop. (My city imagination prone to run wild in dark places, Mike even accompanied me to the outhouse. How's that for gallant?) Perfect meals—whether the menu was thimbleberries and granola at breakfast, crumbled crackers spread with tuna fish for lunch, or dehydrated concoctions for dinner.

Perfect even when we polished off the wine Nalgene, somewhere on the third or fourth day. Because, it turns out, at the end of the day, some things are just as satisfying as a hot shower and a bed. Things like sliding the pack off your shoulders, shedding the hiking boots, and wiggling your toes. Being able to pitch a tent together without talking. Snacking on thimbleberries from a hammock. Playing Scrabble (another untraditional item

I added to the packs) under a flashlight beam.

And on the ferry ride back, when it starts to rain for the first time all week, knowing that next time, you'll know to allocate two Nalgenes for the Merlot.

Cari Noga

Finding a Good Wine ... Shop

Selection

There is an acid test that one can use to determine the breadth of a shop's product line. Look around the store and give it one point for each of the following varieties that are represented. California: Sangiovese, Syrah, Viognier; Oregon: Pinot Gris; France: Reds from Loire, whites from the Rhône; Switzerland: Fendant; Italy: Dolcetto; Argentina: Malbec; South Africa: Pinotage.

0 to 3 Points This is probably a "Liquor Store" rather than a wine shop. The few points it managed to glean were either due to a pushy wine sales rep or a mistaken shipment. Take your business elsewhere!

4 to 7 Points This is an establishment that is at least making a concerted effort to be a fine wine store. If you are on good terms with the proprietor you might diplomatically recommend that he take in a representation of the neglected categories. If he eventually does this—there is hope.

8 to 10 Points Congratulations! Your store has, at least, the breadth of selection to make a great wine shop.

The factor of time comes into play as well. Many good wine stores fail to become truly great wine stores, because they ignore the necessity of adequate bottle age. If a shop doesn't feel they that have the customer base to support the upgrade to a selection of fully-matured bottles, they will create an impressive (but barely drinkable) façade made up of the most current and therefore the least expensive releases. The ideal wine shop should be a place that you can run into on the spur of the moment and grab a palate-pleasing, aged bottle of red for tonight's dinner. If the only serious wine offerings a store has are ones that need to be locked away for fifteen-plus years, they are doing their customers a disservice.

Personnel

Taste is an extremely personal thing, but one of the first things a potential customer should do is ascertain whether the person they will be dealing with sees eye to eye, or in this case tastes bud to bud, regarding what makes an admirable wine.

Ask the wine consultant to recommend a moderately priced red and/or white. (If the individual doesn't query you about what type of food the wine is to go with, or about your general wine preferences, it's a bad sign.) Take the bottles home and see what you think.

When evaluating a bottle, keep in mind how the bottle stacks up against others in this price range. One can't take home a bottle of Chilean Cabernet and upon tasting it muse: Nice, but it's no Haut-Brion. And remember, it is always a lot easier to find an excellent bottle in the higher end of the spectrum than it is to find a simple good value in table wine.

Eric S. Brent

3

RELAXING RENDEZVOUS

Zia Suzy's Fine Wine

The family is the essential presence—
the thing that never leaves you, even
if you find you have to leave it.

Bill Buford

I t was the fine Tuscan spring of 1963. Walking up the mountain road to her home, I saw a tiny woman with chicklet teeth that blazed out of a network of wrinkles. She was completely clothed in black, wild with waving, and the startling blue eyes that jumped out at me were just like my Nonno Enrico's, her brother. She was calling to the neighbors, who were all hanging out of their windows and waving like crazy.

"It's Maria's daughter come to see me! It's Angela and Enrico's granddaughter! It's Isabel!"

I'd heard stories about her my entire life. Then, I was a young teacher with the Army Dependent Schools, stationed in Germany. I'd caught a plane to Florence, gotten a taxi driver to bump up the hills to Montecchio, a jewel of a little village with a front row balcony seat overlooking the fabled city. Its Duomo and ancient spires glittered in the valley distance, while grape vines in neat verdant green rows marched up every hillside. Neighbors exited their cream and yellow homes, painted artistically with vines, and marched out to the street from under more arbors strung with lush varietals planted generations ago. Warm and welcoming, the tight knot of Italians surrounded me smiling, touching me, hugging, some kissing. With a quick gesture, Zia Suzy twined her arm in mine and ushered me into her spacious kitchen where an enormous black aga was heating a kettle for tea. I sat at a wooden table scrubbed for a hundred years, while Suzy, and now my Zio Gussie, fussed. Even with me speaking very little Italian, we managed. They began opening drawers and removing envelopes full of pictures. In the pictures marching across her mantel, I saw my young mother smiling up from the black and whites, my uncle, my grandparents, and even me as a baby. That night, I slept in a gigantic feather bed warmed briefly by a cradle from which hung an iron pot filled with the aga's ashes.

After Nonno and Nonna had emigrated to America for the better life, Suzy, Gussie, and their two tiny daughters had come a year later. Suzy had worked in a Connecticut shirt factory, and Gussie found employment with a family friend who owned a little gas station down the road. They helped in the planting of vino vines around our property, but returned to Italy just a year later, where to them, the better life was waiting. With their American savings, and the sale of their home in the far north of Italy, they moved to the more temperate clime of Tuscany. Proactive and take-charge, Suzy built her own arbors from sturdy logs, began her own vines, dug her own wine cellar, and moved forward towards her own personal destiny that would twine life, vines, and bravery into a story that still lives in Italian history and our minds.

The Second World War came. Zio Gussie was drafted and Suzy was left alone with two teenage daughters. When the German bombing raids became so bad that villages were being leveled, she moved to caves that surrounded Florence and lived there for two years hunting for game, foraging for berries, making her wine, and growing little caches of garden vegetables from the seeds that she could garner from her churned-up house garden. Many caches were buried in the dark of the nights. When the raids ceased, she'd sneak like a fox back to her home and unearth stores, clothing, or other essentials. By then, the town was in ruins, but her arbor and home, while riddled with bullet holes, had escaped total collapse.

At some point, America joined the fray and began strafing missions in hot pursuit of the Germans. On two separate occasions, and perhaps more we never heard about, she and her daughters rescued American flyers by pulling them from their downed planes. She brought them to the caves, hid them, nursed them back to health, spoke to them in the little English she'd gotten in her year in Connecticut and, in complete darkness, guided them by feel of the trail onto mountain trails that eventually lead to the Swiss border or American strongholds.

That 1963 week that I spent with her was rich and full. We took the bus to Florence, and she showed me the city through the eyes of a passionate lover of art, architecture, and food. We ate at little cafés, drank endless cups of espresso, and consumed more red wine than I thought was possible. At one point I broke into song, and the entire place became silent listening. When I was done singing "O Solo Mio," something I'd only treated as a joke, the whole place rose and clapped. I told her all the family stories through a young man she'd found who was studying English in college there. Oh, how she laughed when I told her about Nonno's wine cellar in Connecticut, and the antics of our little family monkey who learned to turn the spigots and suck wine out of Nonno's barrels.

♀ The Secret's Out

The Maremma region of Tuscany, along the Mediterranean coast of Italy, may well become the Napa Valley of Italy. Known for centuries for its Saturnia hot springs and a microclimate similar to Sicily's, it has yet to become a popular destination, although some of the top wine producers, hoteliers, and restaurateurs have invested in the area.

The evening before I left, Zia Suzy and I sat on the old stone wall she's built from the rubble of the war. She hiked her black skirts up around her knees, exposing sturdy lace-up leather mountaineering boots, whose toothy soles were caked with mud. From her wine cellar, a tiny hobbit hole cut into the side of the just greening Tuscan hills, she withdrew a hand-blown green bottle.

"I make and save this for your Mamma," she began, palming an ancient corkscrew. "But, she never come back, and here you are. So, we drink this together. You are a beautiful, beautiful Italian girl. My girl. A singer. A teacher. You do the family proud."

How long the bottle had waited, I never knew. I just knew that after it had bubbled joyfully over the sides, and

Zia Suzy had clapped and cheered its enthusiasm on, she poured the crystal, golden liquid into two cut glass goblets. Her blue eyes locked mine, then broke into a thousand points of light when she swept them over her life, her town, her view, her sky. Together we toasted Florence, the sunset, la famiglia, life, and me. Never before nor since, and never in this lifetime again, I'm sure, will I ever taste a wine so brilliant, so . . . perfect.

Isabel Bearman Bucher

The Connoisseur

A bottle of wine begs to be shared;
I have never met a miserly
wine lover.

Clifton Fadiman

I t must have been the very first thing he spotted while sizing up weight and placement of our belongings. My last gallon of peach chardonnay, perking away in a corner of the garage.

"If you can get to the huckleberries before the bears do, ma'am, they make mighty fine wine," he touted more than once.

Maurice never allowed his yen for the bubbly to interfere with his bon vivant or derelict lifestyles. He mingled comfortably at glitzy, charity wine-tasting parties or sprawled on a park bench, blathering with sack-sipping derelicts. Trusting in God's mercy, he never missed a Sunday at our church, always seated in the balcony, isolated within his own brand of spirits.

Blush-nosed, ruddy-faced Maurice perceived himself a wine aficionado. "A glass or two of the white or red before dinner heightens the appetite and allows for nice uninhibited conversation around any table," he discerned. Trouble was, where there was a wine bottle, there was Maurice rejuvenating his refined palate to excess.

A whopping dose of aftershave hung heavy as he set the packing crew to work directing our departure to Montana. The odd combination permeated the house, glazing over an alcohol stench that seemed to exit from every pore.

"Now, your mom tells me you've been good kids this summer, so here's a lollipop. Oops, and lookie here what I found in the other pocket, a biscuit for the dog," charming his way into the hearts and taste buds of my children.

I hauled the kids and dog to the park for some fresh air and neighborhood farewells after Molly's raucous comments about the smell. I even left a pot of coffee for the guys each morning. In the end, our connoisseur had seen to it that not only was my garbage neatly packaged and taped, but the coffee grounds as well.

The Frenchman bird-dogged his way to the very jugs in which my neighbors and I had brewed vintage berry and fruit wines three years prior. It was a fun fad for us young-marrieds with little money. If a cork fit, any vessel qualified, while tubing gurgled away in laundry rooms, garages, and basements up and down our street. We celebrated New Year's with popping corks and sparkling secondary fermentation that produced perfect spume.

Unhappily, most of us had trouble taming our big jugs of the reds. Despite hours of poring over "how to" manuals, there surfaced a glitch in the process. Instead of fermenting gracefully and sipping like nectar of the gods, the liquor became the stuff of lacquer. Rip-roarin' headaches caused near blindness, and next morning distempers with anyone who dared speak. Even the dog was shushed up.

"No, no, no," Ken barked when I threatened to dump the awful stuff. "We worked hard picking the berries and fruit. Besides, it's very tasty and the guys don't get headaches on poker night."

Across the street, Gladys dispensed her supply into teenage trick or treat bags. The police never darkened her door, so we assumed a bunch of mum kids had a big night somewhere.

 ## Ripe for Harvest

Winemakers measure the Brix (sugar content) and the maturity of the tannins in their grapes to determine when to harvest. A Brix of 23–24 percent is preferred. They then chew on the grape skins and seeds to determine if the tannins have mellowed. If too astringent and pungent, the grapes will hang longer, even if that results in higher sugars.

Georgie sent her fancy bottles incognito to the annual Fireman's Ball at the Elks' Lodge.

Betsy had the nerve to ask Father Andrew if he could use her bitter burgundy at mass. The gracious Father snapped up her three-gallon jugs of crimson offertory, hopefully watered down for communion.

All was packed and trucked, little left besides outdoor furniture and bikes. But there on the garage shelves languished the anvil chorus of red jugs, the things I hoped would mysteriously disappear.

"So long, Campbells," Maurice shouted after us as we drove off to a motel for the night. "Have a wonderful life in Montana, and don't forget those huckleberries and Flathead cherries, Mrs."

"God Almighty," yelled Ken while squinting through the rearview mirror. "I'd know that shock of white hair anywhere. I think Maurice is loading up his pickup with those jugs of wine from the garage! Didn't they get on the van, Kath?"

"Nothing to worry about, dear," assuring him our perfect sparkly was wired tightly and stowed by me personally. "Let Maurice have the headaches and we'll start fresh with Montana's huckleberries and Flathead cherries."

"Sure hope the stuff doesn't kill that nice old man," Ken murmured beneath a devilish grin.

Kathe Campbell

"Your red wine cells are too low."

Night Bloomers Like Cinderella

*I'm like old wine. They don't bring me out
very often, but I'm well preserved.*

Rose Fitzgerald Kennedy

When mornings smell like petunias, and nights envelop us like a warm glove, we know it's almost time. Time to watch for buds on the magical plant—a night-blooming cereus. Sprawling almost out of its container, the plant, which I call Cinderella, sways from a rail on the deck. You'd never suspect its wondrous potential simply by looking at its gawky, leaf-shaped, flattened stems.

Each bud opens for one night only, but what a production. The mysterious blossom starts out as a bud shooting akimbo from a long, floppy leaf. We watch it develop and can usually predict by dusk, the night of its opening. It unfolds to its fullest, about the size of a salad plate, around midnight. The alabaster blossom's petals are tinged with pink, and some people describe the incredible center as a glimpse of heaven itself; others call it "babe in the manger." Opening, the flower exudes an exotic, heady fragrance. The next morning, the blossom dangles limply with little evidence of the previous night's glory.

We always invite a few friends over for wine and cheese, and to watch the flower unfold. They are astounded, especially if they haven't seen this happen before. And so are we—even after seeing it many summers. It's that kind of bloom. Spectacular.

Not everyone wants to attend a spontaneous party, but those who do are always delighted they came—just as I was glad when my neighbor first invited me to witness this phenomenon. I was in the bathtub when she called. "Jump in your pajamas and come on over," she urged. "This is worth it."

Suspended from a tree in the backyard woods line, her potted plant occupied center stage as we sat on lawn chairs to watch. I found it awesome— in the traditional sense of the word. A captivating experience. Soon afterward, I acquired my own plant, or maybe it found me (much like my cat did). The plant had been discarded near the garbage can, awaiting pickup behind my husband's office. I recognized the ugly, gangly foliage with its "rescue me" look. I watched for signs of the enigmatic bloom. Nothing happened that first season. But finally, my vigilance paid off. It bloomed the following August.

Now, it blooms every summer. How, I don't know. During winter months, we keep the plant in the garage by a window, and rarely remember to water it. When spring arrives, we transfer it to the deck, a few steps away from the kitchen door.

Over the years, we've invited some of our favorite people for opening night. Like Leslie, when it bloomed on her birthday. Other visitors include Beth, who brought her favorite wine; Bobbie, who told stories—both tragic and wonderful—as we enjoyed my favorite wine; Carolyn and Bill, who photographed the developing bloom at every stage, and from every angle; and many others. Last year, we invited new neighbors who only recently moved to the South. They were quite taken with the plant, and asked rapid-fire questions—none of which I could answer.

This occasion provides the perfect excuse for an impromptu summer party. We enjoy candlelight, wine, and especially the bond we share with our guests. Cicadas and tree frogs serenade us (often several decibels too loud) as we periodically sweep the flashlight over the bloom to monitor its expansion.

Recently, I read that legendary writer Eudora Welty and some of her friends in Jackson, Mississippi, formed their own Night-Blooming Cereus Club. Their goal was simple—to enjoy an evening of conviviality and celebrate the annual, one-night-only bloom of this exquisite flower.

🍷 *Party Planning*

A bottle of wine contains five, five-ounce servings. Plan for one (5 ounce) glass of wine per wine drinker, per hour. So, for a four hour party, with ten wine drinking guests, you will want to have eight bottles of wine on hand. At a large party, wine drinkers will drink 60 percent white wine to 40 percent red. Have a couple types of white wine on hand; Chardonnay for the enthusiasts, and Pinot Grigio for the rest.

A stellar idea from Miss Welty—and one I'm sure she'd want me to steal. And now, a few steps away, three growing buds promise more miracles soon. We'll watch them with anticipation of a night-blooming cereus party from

10 PM till midnight (later if the people are night bloomers, too). At the appropriate moment the call will go out, "The NBC Club meets tonight. No dues. No rules. Wear your pajamas, a ball gown, or anything in between, your choice. We'll break open that special bottle of Carmenere I brought back from Chile's Colchagua Valley and saved for this occasion."

Gay N. Martin

Anniversary Wine

Wine is a little like love; when the right
one comes along, you know it.

Bolla Wines advertisement

During our honeymoon, my husband and I mean-
dered up the coast of California from Los Angeles
to San Francisco with no plan other than to
indulge ourselves with great food and wine and interesting sights. We'd get up in the morning, decide what we
wanted to do for the day, and then I would call ahead for
a reservation at a bed and breakfast. Some days we drove
for hours. We toured centuries-old adobe churches where
birds nested high in the rafters and you could see the sky
through the ceiling. Other days, we hiked in cool, dim
forests or along golden fields near the ocean.

One particular day, for the first time, I had trouble getting a reservation that night. The guidebook praised a particular bed and breakfast and had given it the highest
rating so I really wanted to stay there. Unfortunately,
there was a corporate retreat in-house and they were
booked solid. "However," paused the sweet young voice
on the phone, "there is a new place that just opened up
down the road. You could see if they have a room." She

gave me the number and wished me good luck. As luck would have it, they had a room available for the night.

We arrived that evening just before 5:30. An elegant, white-haired woman in a sweeping, floral silk dress showed us to our room. She explained that every suite was named for a famous actor and that we were getting the largest, the Douglas Fairbanks suite.

"Dinner is being served at 6:00. We do hope you'll join us down in the parlor to start your evening. My name is Deidre. Let me know if there is anything at all I can do to make your stay perfect for you."

We unpacked quickly, changed our clothes, and headed down the ornately-carved oak staircase. Downstairs, we heard voices from a small room near the front door and joined the other couple. Deidre handed us each a crystal glass of Chardonnay, poured a glass for herself, and proposed a toast to the evening ahead.

The other couple, Lynn and Steve, raised their glasses. "To our fiftieth anniversary!" We toasted them and wished them many more years together.

"And to our first week anniversary!" we laughed. "May we have years together!"

Dierdre excused herself to join her husband, our chef, in the kitchen.

When she returned, we were led into an oak-paneled dining room with five tables covered in snowy white damask tablecloths. Dierdre showed Lynn and Steve to a table near the fireplace because Lynn felt a chill. We took seats near the French doors, hung with generous drapes, leading to a stone terrace. Vivaldi played quietly in the background.

Dierdre's husband, Mark, a huge, dark-bearded man in chef's toque and immaculate apron, strode through an upholstered door into the dining room. "I understand there are anniversaries here tonight. For you, I have prepared a magnificent meal!"

Behind him Dierdre carried a small silver tray with six tiny, crystal glasses filled with amber liquid. "For the anniversaries, all the anniversaries—past, present, and to come!" She placed a glass before each of us, handed one to her husband, and raised her own.

The meal was one of the best my husband and I have shared during our twenty-five years of marriage, and we toasted each other many times that night. Lynn and Steve smiled at us fondly, asked us questions about New York City where we lived, and told us about their grandchildren. We wished Deidre and Mark the best of luck with their dream of owning a successful bed and breakfast.

Every anniversary since we have opened a special bottle of amber anniversary wine to toast our good fortune in having each other and so many wonderful memories to cherish.

Louise Foerster

Ecology and the Grape

Millions of years ago, the north and south downs of southern England were joined with the champagne region of France. Both regions share the same geology and nutrients in the soil, and have south-facing slopes to provide maximum sunlight.

Climate change, bringing long, intense, hot summers, is heralding abundant grape crops and some of the finest wine in the world—in England. Even the great French champagne houses are looking to buy or establish their own vineyards in southern England.

Several wineries in California, an ecologically progressive state, have "gone green." The historic Parducci Wine Cellars make delicious wine, and do the right things to make a healthier planet. From tree-free papers and soy-based inks, to biodiesel tractors and organic grape growing, Parducci is creating a model of quality and environmental sustainability for other wineries to follow.

Frog's Leap wines are produced from grapes grown on John Williams's organic farm in Rutherford. John's entire winery is solar-powered, and is heated and cooled geothermally. His tasting room and offices are LEED-certified by the U.S. Green Building council and are built with renewable, low-impact materials. Better yet, Frog's Leap wines are delicious.

If you are an environmentally conscious wine lover, the EcoVine Wine Club in Santa Barbara, California, specializes in finding wines grown organically without pesticides, fungicides, synthetic fertilizers, or chemicals of any kind.

No Wrath in These Grapes

The real point of wine is to satisfy
the thirst that comes with eating. This is how
it is drunk by those working in the vineyards,
as an accompaniment to food, an
additional flavoring, a liquid condiment.

Emile Peynaud

J ustin and Shirley's vineyard is in a valley
between two ranges of hills, and their magnificent home sits on a bluff overlooking the vineyard. After passing through a gate you travel about half a
mile uphill to the house and all its comforts. My wife and
I spent our forty-ninth wedding anniversary here the year
before, and Justin invited me to return in October to help
with the harvest. Nicholas, the German Shepherd, and the
two vineyard cats, Mama Cat and her son Super Boy, wel-
comed me back.

The day after I arrived was spent getting ready. We
serviced the three tractors and their trailers and the forklift. We replaced or repaired water hoses, sharpened the
curved knives, and got ready for the arrival of the grape
pickers. Early the next foggy morning, twenty-six
seasoned vineyard workers reported for duty. Only the

foreman spoke some English, and I made a silent, solemn promise to learn some Spanish before the next harvest. These were all experienced harvesters, and they quickly broke up into three teams and went right to work.

One man was designated to operate the fork lift, and two men and one woman were selected to drive the three diesel-powered tractors. Each tractor pulled a trailer carrying three large bins, each of which could hold a half-ton of grapes.

The tractor started down between two rows of grapes, followed by the pickers, who would push a plastic basket with their feet while busily using the knives to cut the grape clusters, which once free, dropped into the basket. They were very adept, and the baskets filled quickly and were dumped into the bins on the trailer. When the three bins were filled, the tractor proceeded to a concrete slab where the forklift waited to lift the bins and dump them into four large vats sitting on two large flatbed trailers pulled by a diesel truck.

Each of the four vats had a capacity of six tons of grapes. When the four vats were filled, the truck delivered the grapes to a winery in Paso Robles where they would eventually wind up as a bottle of Cabernet Sauvignon in about two years. The operation went on for two days and resulted in fifty tons of grapes shipped to the winery.

Justin kept two tons for his own small family boutique winery located in a building on the vineyard grounds. I watched the preparation for wine-making very closely so I would be more of an asset next year. The clusters of grapes were dropped into a trough with a revolving screw auger in it. It drops the grapes into one basket, and the stems into another. The basket of grapes are emptied into a vat that holds a ton of the small, dark purple, sweet-and-juicy globes. The stems are ground up and used to fertilize the vines. Nothing is wasted.

The grapes are crushed with a long-handled, stainless-steel masher. No longer do you dance on the grapes with purple feet. Next, vintners yeast is added, and the vats are covered to allow the yeast to change fructose into alcohol. When the alcohol level gets high enough, the yeast cells die, and then the juice is strained and moved by hose to the bottom floor of the winery, into the oak barrels which are stored in the cool wine cellar at fifty-five degrees.

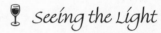

Seeing the Light

The Foss Winescan Analyzer projects a beam of infrared light through wine or juice, and can identify over eighteen components based on their ability to absorb light. This new tool gives vintners greater control over the vinification process and increases consistency in their wines.

After aging in the oak for eighteen to twenty-four months, the wine will be ready for bottling and will join the other ten thousand bottles in racks covering all the walls of the cellar. The two tons of grapes Justin kept for his winery will make about 200 cases of wine. The 2001 vintage would be a good one because the sugar content (Brix) of the grapes was higher than usual.

Justin gave me a case of wine to bring home. It was a case of his 1997 Cabernet Sauvignon, a very special vintage. Each year I went back to the vineyard to help with the harvest. I always arrived more knowledgeable than the year before, and left understanding how much more there was to learn about this art of wine making. My good friend Justin E. Marshall died in May 2006, at age seventy-eight. One of the last things he did was to bottle some special wine with my name on the label. I will treasure every drop.

Harry Rubin

Make an Impression

Need a "thank-you" gift for clients? Want to commemorate a significant milestone in your company's history or growth? How about a unique fund-raising item for your alumni association or nonprofit organization?

Signature Wines takes a bottle of fine wine to the next level, adding a personal touch that gets noticed. They will custom-label premium and specialty wines to create a unique gift as a tool to build relationships, generate brand recognition, and even increase revenue. Wines are sourced from some of the best wineries of California.

Wines that could make a lasting impression are:

- Pesquera 2001 Ribera del Duero Crianza from the Rioja region of Spain. Made from the Tinto Fino, a local variety of Tempranillo, it has a black cherry color and is well balanced.

- Conundrum is a dramatically different white-wine blend that surpasses the scope of single-varietal wines. This wine's complexity makes it appealing to both red and white drinkers.

- An Argentinian Malbec, such as the 2003 Familia Cassone Luján de Cuyo Obra Prima Reserva, is a big, robust red that definitely makes a statement.

- A Greek wine that would be on the ultimate wine lover's wish list would be the Argyros 1984 Santorini Vin Santo.

A Turn of the Corkscrew

A Book of Verses underneath the Bough,
A Jug of Wine, a Loaf of Bread—and Thou
Beside me singing in the Wilderness—
Oh, Wilderness were Paradise enow!

Omar Khayyám

I n desperation, on the day of my wife's birthday (which one, I'm not at liberty to say), I'd made a reservation at The French Café, a bistro of sorts which, at the time, languished on Michigan Avenue near Balbo at the south end of the Loop in Chicago. I knew nothing about it except its name and location. I didn't have great hopes, either, but to paraphrase Holmes, with everything else being impossible, the improbable became the solution to the problem of where to celebrate the occasion.

We found parking nearby, no small accomplishment in itself, but could not find The French Café, neither a block north, nor a block south of the address. We did find Bumbershoot. My last best hope for a touch of Gallic savoir faire in the jungle of downtown Chicago had turned will-o'-the-wisp. Bumbershoot, your basic blue plate special businessman's semi-upscale eatery, seemingly had pushed its predecessor off its concrete base and taken its place.

What can I tell you? I confessed all to my spouse, who forgave me and suggested we sate our sorrows with a plate of pasta and whatever variety of Gallo or similar the establishment offered.

Bumbershoot proved a clean, well-lighted place with two waiters to service about eight tables, only one of which was occupied—ours. The food was serviceable, if unremarkable, but surprisingly well prepared.

And, then, there was the wine. Ah, the wine!

We asked about wine and the waiter went off to consult with his colleague. Then, the two went into the kitchen for a while. Then, the chef emerged and explained that they'd opened only a few days before and hadn't stocked any wine, not having expected their customers to be oenophiles, even of the neophyte variety. But, said the chef, the restaurant he'd bought out had left quite a bit of wine in the cellar. If we liked, he'd bring up a couple of bottles and we could choose.

Know When to Fold 'Em

Two avid collectors, bidding against each other, got carried away at an auction in New York. When the gavel fell, the winning bid was $167,500 for a lot of seven bottles of a Montrachet 1978 from Domaine de la Romanée-Conti, the most expensive bottles of still-drinkable wine ever auctioned.

I don't remember what the other was, but we chose the '59 Château La Tache; wine as brilliant as cut crystal, red as a cabochon ruby, an almost musky bouquet that turned flinty and fruity by turns. It was a gossamer of silk unfolding on and enveloping, the palate, a fragrance not of the nose only but of the entire olfactory-gustatory apparatus. And so we dawdled our way to the end of a meal made incomparable by an incomparable wine, easily the best it has been our pleasure to quaff.

Oh, yes, the bill. I haven't the slightest idea what the meal cost but the wine came to ten dollars, and the chef apologized, saying he had no idea what to charge. Today, its equivalent would probably exceed $700. We have one regret—we didn't offer to buy the cellar then and there.

Stuart Jay Silverman

Sharing the Cup of Life

I would rather have a mind
opened by wonder than one
closed by belief.

Gerry Spence

I come from Methodist stock. My people are responsible for Thomas Welch, a man who so fervently believed wine should not pass people's lips in church that he invented grape juice. As a child, I so absorbed Welch's stance that I believed alcohol worked like a sinister spell, turning potentially kind souls into lewd creatures. My impression changed the day I took my first sip.

I can't remember exactly how a bottle of wine got into my house. Maybe someone new to Methodism wrapped it up as a Christmas gift for my minister father, thinking you can't go wrong with a bottle of wine. Maybe it came in a gift basket from the town funeral director. Either way, it sat on our pantry shelf for a year: the forbidden fruit. In our culture, drinking was clearly uncouth, so I couldn't believe it when one evening my father took the bottle from our pantry shelf and brought it to the living room.

"Shall we drink it?" he asked.

He might as well have said, "Shall I quit my job and start a new career as one of those guys who runs sideshows in the circus?"

"Yes," I said.

Dad disappeared into the kitchen and returned with a tray of our finest teacups. Ceremoniously, he passed them out to my mother, my brother, and me. Commemorative words seemed appropriate, but instead one of us said, "One, two, three."

Cautiously, I lifted the wine to my lips. I held it on my tongue for a moment, and then, feeling ready, I gave it the go-ahead to roll down my throat. I'm not sure what I thought would happen. Mindless stupor? A wild craving to drain the bottle? A compelling urge to perform a dance on my father's roll-top desk? Nothing compromising followed my first sip, so I took a second, and a third. Somewhere in there, I felt a tingle. It spread down my spine to my fingertips. I kept this to myself, since I didn't know what others were feeling, and thought it might indicate a special aptitude for debauchery.

Staring at the fireplace, I practiced my move-along-there's-nothing-to-see-here look as the bubbly sensation spread toward my toes. Finally, my mother said, "I'm starting to feel something."

♟ *Spiritual Roots*

Wine and religion are inextricably intertwined. Wine is mentioned 155 times in the Old Testament and 10 times in the New. Christian monasteries dominated wine production for thousands of years until the French Revolution, when vineyards were taken from the Church and redistributed to the people, effectively secularizing wine.

We sipped more until the bubbly feeling gave way to the subtly more expansive, subtly more loving feeling. I couldn't believe that was what we'd protected ourselves from all those years.

I'd been right about one thing: After the cork came out of the bottle, there was no going back. Not because I couldn't resist an urge, but because I saw that I had based my prohibitionist beliefs on false assumptions.

These days, my once-wagon-riding father owns a "support your local brewery" T-shirt that he discretely wears on vacations. He got it after graduating from the brewery's beer appreciation class.

As for me, I still enjoy an occasional glass of wine. Given the sedentary nature of my profession, I feel it's a healthy alternative to too much chocolate cake. What I enjoy even more than the wine is being able to celebrate life wholeheartedly with a wider circle of friends than before—to raise my glass in a tradition as ancient as the Egyptian god Osiris or even dance arm-in-arm with giddy strangers in a vat of fermented grapes.

Re-examining sacred beliefs is never painless, but looking back, I'm glad we opened the bottle.

Laura Marble

Thanks for the Memories

Give me books, fruit, French wine and fine
weather and a little music out of doors,
played by someone I do not know.

John Keats

Into every life, memories fall, some as gentle as
spring rain, others that bury us under the
proverbial load of bricks, and most of mine were
made—and toasted—with wine.

A cup of warmed, sweet Mogan David helped me sleep
through a head cold at seven. A year later, sitting proud in
a puffy pink Easter dress, I felt oh-so-grown-up when I
was allowed to sip watered-down Gallo from a slim-
stemmed goblet instead of a tumbler. The toast eleven-
year-old me practiced for my favorite uncle's wedding
was supposed to go, "May misfortune follow you the rest
of your lives . . . and never catch up!" But after a glass of
undiluted home-made vino, "May you be misfortunate
forever!" is what I slurred into the microphone.

I didn't touch the stuff for years after that, though there
was always at least one bottle under the kitchen sink at
home and at Nonna's house.

Already-of-age college pals helped me celebrate my

twenty-first birthday with a bottle of Chablis. Older and wiser, I'd learned patience (and portioning), and woke the next day an adult in the eyes of the law, alert and smiling, and headache free.

When I married the man of my dreams at twenty-two, we performed the "linked wrists" trick for wedding guests without spilling a drop of Bollinger. That night, alone in our honeymoon "suite" we polished off the enormous bottle of wine provided by our hotel. Our theory? If we remained tipsy enough, we wouldn't complain to the manager about the reservations snafu that put us in a small room—with twin beds.

Over the years, and glasses of wine, my beloved and I celebrated birthdays and anniversaries, toasted the births of our daughters, his pay raises and promotions, my book sales, the girls' graduations. We cried into our wine at their weddings—me, because our little girls weren't little girls any more, he because caterers and bandleaders and banquet hall managers awaited payment—and again when they presented us with bald-but-beautiful grandchildren.

When a storm blew off a section of roof, shingles and boards weren't the only things damaged: Photographs, diplomas and degrees, hand-crafted Mothers' Day cards, and numerous other precious memorabilia were ripped from our lives by the brutal grip of the howling wind or drowned in the driving rain. And wine took some of the sting from our anguished loss.

Wine's cordiality—from a vineyard's label to the foxy-fruity vintage inside round-shouldered green, brown, or black glass bottles—has always been the perfect one-size-fits-all gift for housewarmings, christenings, thank-yous, and congratulations.

I'm hard pressed to name a country that doesn't boast special wine-growing talents. Wine's rich history, with roots in the Neolithic Period, has been integral to religious ceremonies, family customs, recipes, songs, movies, and books. It is synonymous with deliverance, redemption, freedom, protection, and passion. Each occasion, every celebration earmarked "special" by wine's presence becomes all the more memorable.

♀ Some Like It Hot

The volcanic Atlantic island of Madeira, part of Portugal, is famous for its wine's distinctive flavor, which is the result of a special heating process. Casks are either stored in warm lofts over several years or heated in concrete or stainless steel tanks. Because of this heat exposure, Madeiras will drink well from an opened bottle for a number of weeks, even months. Madeira was a favorite wine of Thomas Jefferson's, and a bottle from his wine cellar sold for $20,000 in 1997.

What fun it is, showing off our knowledge of "wine terms" in restaurants! But whether we can differentiate between supple and stale, toasty or tinny, if the bottle on our table cost seven or seven hundred dollars, the palatability of wine is as universally recognized as a smile.

So, I raise my glass to wine of every shade and age, and join Bing Crosby in his rich rendition of *Thanks for the Memories*.

Loree Lough

Communion Wine

The family is one of nature's masterpieces.

George Santayana

"Paisano" is a very dry, red wine that Dad used to buy by the gallon. It was a cheap, but satisfying wine. Throughout the years, I had many pleasant memories of sipping Paisano with my family. We often drank a small glass with dinner. Dad would pour for everyone while Mom bustled about the kitchen, trying to get the meal on the table before it got cold.

Because of those happy times, I reached for Paisano wine to toast my Dad's memory when his life was ebbing away. The night before he died, I uncorked a bottle and took a long drink of that delicious dry wine. I'd just come home from my Dad's bedside at my parents' house, visiting him, holding his hand, and speaking love to him. The hospice nurse had informed us that his end was near. Mom and other family members were seated by him, keeping watch. They suggested I go back to my own place and rest. There was nothing else I could do, they assured me, and my husband needed me at home.

So I kissed Dad goodnight, then drove to the suburban ranch home that I share with my husband and two cats.

As I collapsed in an armchair, memories from the past flooded over me. I needed to revel in those memories, so I turned to a bottle of Paisano red wine, our favorite family wine that made me feel good every time I drank it.

"Dad! I'm going to miss you so much!" I whispered those words into the heavy silence of my living room. My father was going to die within a day or two. Never again would he stride through my front door, stopping by to swap the latest family news. I felt battered by pain. Still, I knew Dad would want me to stay strong. So I filled a glass and raised it in the air. It felt like a special moment to me, almost like I was taking Communion.

When I was a little girl, Dad and I used to stand in line together at church to take Communion. As I sat in that armchair, I recalled the purpose of that holy rite. After a minute of silent meditation, I drank down my glass of Paisano, feeling like I was saluting Dad in the same holy spirit. I knew that somehow, he and I were communing through this wine. I sensed an aura of peace pass over me. I wondered if Dad was feeling the Lord's peace, also.

Six weeks later, at Easter time, a nun from church visited Mom's home to serve us Communion. Mom wasn't getting out much because she was still recovering from the stress of losing Dad. Partaking of the elements made me think of Dad, and I realized that the pain of his loss was growing less, while the good memories were getting stronger. Later that evening, I poured Mom and myself a glass of Paisano and we relaxed over a plate of kielbasa, sauerkraut, and hard rolls. "Let's toast Dad again, for old time's sake," I suggested.

Mom's eyes twinkled. "You think he's watching us, don't you? Watching us from above."

"Yeah, I do." In fact, I felt sure of it. And I sensed that this ritual would spiritually connect Mom and me to Dad, and the peace that he was surely experiencing in his eternal rest. I raised my glass, and Mom raised hers. We clinked glasses, and it felt so right.

Joyce Uhernik Kurzawski with Cheryl Elaine Williams

Wines to Try

Reds

Red Guitar 2005 Tempranillo Garnacha, Northern Spain. These grapes are grown between Bordeaux and Rioja, a region that has grown grapes since the time of the ancient Romans.

Columbia Crest "Grand Estates" Cabernet Sauvignon 2002 from the Columbia Valley, Washington. You'll enjoy rich cassis, cedar, and mocha.

J. C. Cellars Ventana Vineyard Syrah 2002 from Monterey, California, offers smoky and earthy tones with dark berries and black pepper.

Whites

Alexander Valley Vineyards "New Gewurz" Gewurztraminer 2005 from North Coast, California. Flavors of lively apple with honeysuckle and tasty minerals.

Talley Vineyards Estate Chardonnay 2004 from Arroyo Grande Valley, California, serves up spicy apple crisp flavors with a long, creamy finish.

Sparkling

Ballatore Rosso Red Spumante is an inexpensive sparkling red from California. Its fruity flavors and aromas make it a perfect choice for Valentine's Day.

Piper-Heidsieck's new Cuvée Sublime has a hint of sweetness that makes it a luxurious complement to a range of hors d'oeuvres and desserts.

"Yes," one woman replied, and a smile warmed her face. "Go up the street," she said in that decidedly Caribbean lilt, pointing to a footpath worn in the grass between low, tin-roofed houses. "It's a two-story building."

My son ran ahead, happy to be on land. Lights glowed in some of the houses. An unseen radio played music loudly. Skidding to a halt before a two-story building, my son shouted that he'd found it. He seemed unaware that there were differences between where we were walking and where we lived. To him, these were houses, a street, rock and roll, a grocery store. No different.

A couple of young girls outside the store ducked their heads shyly but managed a "hi" when I spoke to them.

Inside, plastic crates of glass soda bottles rose in stacks from the floor. A wooden counter separated us from a few narrow wooden boards nailed to the wall, lined with canned and bottled goods. Bare light bulbs flickered over the goods and the heavy-set proprietress as she emerged from a back room, a dishcloth in her hands.

"Can I help you?" she asked.

A glance around proved wine wasn't part of her stock. But I couldn't think what else to say.

"Do you have any wine?" I asked.

"Oh, no," she laughed, tilting her head back, delighted by the joke. Then she stopped mid-chuckle and raised an amused eyebrow. "What kind?"

I was confused. "Red, white, whatever you have . . . ?"

"Oh no," she repeated. "We don't have anything like that. But we have homemade wine." She looked at me as if it were a test of some sort—not a challenge, but a simple question to see, perhaps, what type of tourists we really were.

I must have looked surprised. "Homemade wine?"

"Yes," she replied, drawing out the word into syllables only heard in the Caribbean, pulling it along before me like a string before a kitten. "But not here. My daughter will show you." Her infectious smile made me relax a little and laugh, too.

"Sure, that sounds . . . interesting," I managed.

The girl led us, without talking, past multicolored houses and chickens scratching in the lush grass, to a large, open building near the shore. A figure jumped up from a group of men sitting on chairs and upturned boxes, and disappeared into the building ahead of us.

Inside, a long wooden picnic table, a well-worn pool table, and two lawn chairs looked lost in the empty room. A giant moth danced around a bare light bulb. On the far side of the building, a half door separated a storage room from the main room, and the man we'd seen stood behind it. The bartender.

The girl whispered in a language I didn't recognize, and he lit up. He showed me a bottle I recognized as a local rum brand, with an inch of pale amber liquid in it. "I'll be right back," he said, and vanished out the main door into the darkness.

♀ A Good Investment?

Over a twelve-year period, the value of the world's most exclusive Bordeaux wines only appreciated half as quickly as the major stock indexes. The upside? If you don't see the appreciation you desire, you can always drink to your losses.

When he reappeared, he presented me with the now-full bottle. Then he had a thought. "Would you like to try it?" he asked, and pulled a disposable cup from its cellophane.

With Aija watching warily, I braced myself for turpentine. But it was sweet and light—a little like white zinfandel. "This is good," I assured him, and he grinned. "Did you make it?"

He nodded.

"What kind is it?"

"Rice wine," he said, clearly proud.

We asked him how much it was, and we paid him the Belizean equivalent of three U.S. dollars.

Later, as Aija and I sat with our husbands on the sailboat, the bottle of wine sitting before us like a centerpiece, Aija said, "I can't believe you drank that. How do you know where the water to make it came from?" Her question was valid.

But I did know where the water came from. It came from that muddy river where crocodiles hide, and herons wade. Where howler monkeys roar, and jaguars stalk, and where women upstream still slap their laundry on flat rocks. It came from a village that was blown flat by Hurricane Iris in 2001, but that was rebuilt by villagers whose parents and grandparents had weathered similar storms in earlier days. It came from the hands of a winemaker with a genuine smile who is proud of his craft, and who opens his bar to locals and North American tourists alike. It came from a place that couldn't be more different from the place we lived, filled with people just like us.

For three dollars, I was reminded that traveling is more than scenery.

And all because we were looking for wine.

Kelley J. P. Lindberg

Is That All I Get?

Good wine is a good familiar creature, if it
be well used.

William Shakespeare, Othello

"I'm carrier qualified!"

My husband and his fellow Navy student pilots had flown out over the Gulf of Mexico and successfully landed on an aircraft carrier. It was the most exciting and grueling part of their Navy flying careers to date, making them members of an exclusive worldwide "club." Only five percent of pilots in the world can accomplish landing on a ship bobbing in the ocean.

Celebration automatically followed at the elegant Officers' Club on the main base in Pensacola, Florida. We were young and thrilled, not used to such extravagances, since we lived with hardly two dimes to rub together during the flight-training period. We were "broke but not poor," my husband was fond of saying.

Sitting by the bay, the O'Club looked like an elegant, white antebellum home, and I was awestruck that we would actually be going inside. The front awning led us through an arched doorway into a massive lobby. Double doors to the right opened to a dark paneled bar, but the revelers had filled it and spilled out into the lobby. Young men swarmed everywhere chanting, "I'm carrier qualified!" while hoisting their beers and celebrating boisterously.

Across the hall on the left, French doors led to an elegant dining room, complete with crystal chandeliers, tables adorned with linen cloths, silver, crystal, fine china, and fresh flowers arranged in silver Revere bowls. Those few young men who were married opted for dinner there with their wives. We joined another couple and headed through those doors for the first time. As we were seated, Molly and I were quite nervous, but my Bill and her husband Dick were glowing with pride.

"Shall we order a bottle of wine?" Bill asked.

"Sure—you earned it!" Molly and I said, almost in unison.

"Okay, what kind? I don't know anything about wine." He reached for a leather-covered small book that sat on the table. "Let's find one on the list that we can afford."

Dick summoned the waiter, a mature, genteel gentleman who served with grace and competence and wore a white dress coat and tie. He treated us as if we were royalty and offered us hors d'oeuvres arranged in a flat, oval silver dish that included marinated fresh tuna, celery, carrots, enormous green and black olives, and radishes cut to look like flowers. We nibbled, chatted as we relaxed, sipped our water, and waited for the wine.

Soon our waiter reappeared with a silver bucket filled with ice and set it by Dick's chair. He then showed him the label and proceeded to open the bottle, handing him the cork. Wiping the rim of the bottle with a linen napkin, which he then wrapped around the neck of the bottle, he poured half an inch of wine in Dick's glass.

Dick looked at the wine. Then at the waiter. Again he stared at his glass, glanced at Bill, then looked up at the waiter and said, "Is that all I get?"

Without a sound, the waiter bowed slightly, filled Dick's glass and then poured each of ours. "Enjoy," he said as he placed the half-empty bottle in the ice bucket and backed away.

Never was there any sign of amusement on his face, nor a word, not even one of instruction. He and his coworkers must have had a great laugh later.

Through the years we've learned about wine, how to drink it, how to choose it. We've traveled with friends to wineries in Germany and California, and have developed a taste for our favorites. Rarely are we served, though, without giving each other a private small smile of remembrance, and one of us whispering, "Is that all I get?"

Jean Stewart

🍷 *Two-Wheeling Tours*

Every year the Northern California Chapter of the National Multiple Sclerosis Society organizes the "Waves to Wine Bike Tour." In September 2006, more than 1,500 cyclists biked 150 miles over two days through Napa and Sonoma counties, enjoying breathtaking views of the wine country and Pacific Coast. Since its inception in 1985, the tour has raised nearly $9 million.

Of Wine, Women, and Song

A person needs at intervals to
separate from family and companions
and go to new places. One must go
without familiars in order to be open
to influences, to change.

Katharine Butler Hathaway

I began to drink wine because of the sophistication attached to it. As a young Indian woman, I was brought up to understand the perils of drinking. Drinking alcohol led to alcoholism, there were no two ways about it. And as any teenager will tell you, that which is forbidden needs to be tried and tested. So while in college, I started with beer. I liked it once I got over its bitterness, but it made me rather sleepy. Then I tried rum which I loved with coke, but gave up because it became too sweet a drink for my fast developing taste buds. I hated the approved ladies drink, a gin and tonic, not because it came attached with the hangover that India has about doing everything the British way, but because it gave me a headache every time I decided to drink it.

However, all in all, despite the admonitions and the frowns from the staid grown-ups, I enjoyed alcohol. I learned soon enough how to have it in the moderate amount that suited my constitution without falling into an alcoholic stupor, making a mess of myself, or creating a scene in public which would have been very detrimental both to my system and my reputation.

The problem was that I had had enough of beer, rum, and whisky, and growing up now, found them not quite my style. It was natural then that I turn to wine. Women could drink its ruby-red splendor in their long, ruby-red, velvet gowns with rubies on their throat and red lipstick on their sensuous mouths. The picture was so enticing that I fell in love with the concept long before I took my first sip of wine.

♈ what's your wine?

Think speed dating for the single set with a new twist: wine-tasting dating. Events combine an assortment of wines and members of the opposite sex in a relaxed atmosphere where guests blind-taste wine and then guess what they are drinking with each partner. At the very least, it's a fun way to learn about wine, and possibly find your soul mate.

Though I identified wine drinking with all things glamorous, the first time I drank red wine was while traveling in Goa in a ramshackle Gypsy van with my family and cousins.

Unlike in the rest of India, wine is available easily in Goa. We had packed in bottles of wine and walnut 'feni" to take as gifts for people back home. My sister-in-law and I, the two more adventurous women on the scene, decided that when in Goa, we must taste the wine as well. After all, we should know what we were taking home for the others. We were, however, wary of opening any bottle to take a taste, lest we devour everything (if we liked it), or waste it (if we did not).

Wine was also being sold in small pouches at roadside stalls, so both of us went ahead and bought a couple of pouches. We had to make a hole at the corner of a pouch and then suck on it, squeezing the bottom of the pouch while doing so. There were no straws available. Soon enough, our husbands were told to replenish our stock, or the bottles would be opened. By the time we crossed the border, my sister-in-law and I were happily singing, a pouch in hand and some purple stains on our clothes. At the state border, the police let us whiz past them with the politeness they show women traveling with their families.

I slurped wine from the small disposable pouches, sang happily into the sunshine as the van rattled its way on the rough road, my arms around my sister-in-law, and now wine-drinking buddy. In Goa, I was introduced to the pleasures of wine in circumstances quite different from the ones I had envisaged.

I have had wine thereafter at social gatherings. Dressed in a stylish sari, I have sipped it decorously in gold-trimmed goblets and proceeded to make polite conversation. This is in keeping with my concept of wine drinking, and its portrayal in coffee-table magazines. I may be doing it in vain, or being vain in my attempts to do so, but I do try to live up to this image of sophistication when I drink my wine. My own experience has shown, though, that wine can be enjoyed in diverse situations. All it needs is the right spirit!

Abha Iyengar

Fruit of the Vine

Take wine seriously but not yourself.

Erik Liedholm, Sommelier

The day I said "I do," I should have declared, "We do, and could you pass the wine?"

On September 30, 2000, my husband and I combined our families for a total of eight children, blended like fine wine. After a month honeymooning in Italy, where we were inspired by the vineyards we had toured, we returned home to a beautiful Indian summer and the end of a summer drought.

The only plants that had survived were the grapes, which were so abundant that branches drooped heavily into the parched grass. My husband, Dino, smiled and declared, "We are going to have to make wine this year!" Ironically, even though neither of us had ever made wine before, we owned a wine press. We had just spent a month in Italy, we liked to drink wine, and we had a book. How hard could it be?

Our wine-making book became like another appendage. "At harvest time, pick the fruit on a sunny day when the sugars flow to the skin," it read. The day of picking the grapes I gathered my two white, five-gallon buckets and my blue-handled scissors, and went off into the beautiful cloudless day. The sun warmed my skin, and the fruit, releasing the most heady fragrance from the grapes. It was an intoxicating experience. I lost all sense of time as I tossed the sticky fruits of the vine into the white containers accompanied by the sound of bees and flies droning around me.

Time! Oh, no! The kids . . . football practice . . . soccer . . . dinner! Hurriedly, I gathered my harvest, banging the buckets against my grape-stained legs, brushing off the bees and flies. I dropped my treasure in the shade as the phone rang.

"Hi Babe, I just wanted to tell you that I am working late and won't be home for dinner, and I love you. Did you get the grapes picked?"

"Yes," I grumbled back, looking at my watch, knowing the kids would be running laps at practice for being late.

Feeling overwhelmed, I grabbed the book and headed to practice. Later, sitting on the hard bleachers with the sound of the coaches' whistles blowing in the background, I read. "When the grapes ripen, you might have to drop everything and go get them on short notice, often in the middle of the week." Wine-making seemed to parallel our family life, from the messy de-stemming process to the traumatic pressing of the grapes.

Our grapes brewed and bubbled through that first Thanksgiving and Christmas of our lives together. As a surprise, Dino had a bottle professionally corked and set aside for our first anniversary. When we celebrated that year, he poured us each a glass and we sipped it liked the masters. We smelled the rich bouquet, and I was transported back to the day of the harvest.

Again I tasted the sweetness of the grapes, felt the warmth of the sun on my shoulders, heard the droning of the bees, and the rustle of the dry grass beneath my feet. I took another sip. Memories of our first year together mingled with the fruits of our labor. I sensed something complex, intriguing, somewhat mystical. Something that hadn't been described in our book, something we discovered as we became a family that year—that love has a way of perfecting the blending process, whether it be grapes or families.

Carolyn Boni

West Coast Domination

The United States ranks fourth behind France, Spain, and Italy in wine production. California is the #1 wine producing state, accounting for over 50 percent of the nation's wineries. Washington State is #2, boasting more than 400 vintners, 350 viticulturalists, and 30,000 vineyard acres.

A Toast to Friendship

A single rose can be my garden . . .
a single friend, my world.

Leo Buscaglia

I sink into a canvas beach chair and stretch tired legs along the cedar planks of the deck. My husband, Ray, and I are houseguests of dear friends Bob and Dorothy. Their beach house is nestled in Neskowin, Oregon, a charming little town of weathered cottages, wind-blown pines, and colorful, well-tended gardens. Leif and Anna Swenson, good friends too, complete our sextet. We've just had an enjoyable, but challenging, bicycle ride up over Cape Lookout along the Oregon Coast.

Bob hands out wine glasses and begins to pour. "It's a Pinot," he says. "A symbol of our friendship."

"Hear, hear," Dorothy adds, touching all our glasses with hers.

"Not that I don't love both you, and a good Pinot," I say, "but a Pinot Noir can't actually be a symbol of our friendship." Writers quibble about things like this.

"Hold that thought," Dorothy says. "I love a good argument. But we need something to go with our wine." She steps into the house and returns with a bowl of clam dip and a bag of chips.

"The six of us and a Pinot grape have nothing in common," I say when she returns.

"Sure we do." Bob takes a sip of his wine and holds it in his mouth for several seconds before letting it slide down his throat. "Think about it. A Pinot is full-bodied and rich, but not heavy. Just like Dorothy." He winks at Dorothy and mouths a kiss.

We all laugh. Bob and Dorothy have been married more than forty years, but someone watching them would think they were caught in the pink cloud stage of early dating.

"Okay," I say. "One for you. But I remember reading somewhere that the Pinot grape is genetically unstable. No matter what the attributes of the vine, one never knows exactly what a grape is going to turn out like. We, on the other hand, can bike together season after season with confidence that Bob will lead, Dorothy will put away the miles, Ray will pass me on every hill, I'll outride him on the flat, Anna will be the sweep, and Leif will take every side road we come to, but be back very soon to report. Afterward we'll have a fabulous happy hour, with lots of wine and jokes, and maybe even a semi-serious discussion about something. It's the same every time."

"Or, one might say that Leif is genetically unstable," Dorothy says with a smile. "At least when he rides a bike."

Leif laughs heartily "I'm just a stumble-on-my-own-shadow type of guy. On the other hand, life is boring if you just bike the beaten path. You miss the Osprey nests, the interesting manhole covers . . ."

"Interesting manhole covers? Is that why you turned yourself upside down this morning?" Bob asks. "Quite a sight, you on your back with your bike still clipped on above you."

"Actually, I slowed down to talk to a couple I saw on the road, and I forgot to pedal enough to stay upright. So me and the Pinot, we're soul brothers."

"And another thing," Bob says. "Pinots supposedly take on the flavor of the soil where the vines are grown. I'd say we're doing a pretty good job of taking on the flavor of this place."

I look through my bare toes at the waves rolling lazily onto shore, trimming the sand with a line of white lace as they recede. The breeze that usually comes up in the afternoon has chosen to blow elsewhere, and the August sun is warm on our faces. At home we're all so busy it takes half a dozen e-mail rounds to schedule a get-together. Here our most ambitious effort, other than a daily bike ride, is solving a Sudoku.

♈ On Par with the Best

The northern Coastal range of Oregon enjoys long hours of summer sunshine and the occasional marine breeze, which keeps the climate moderate and allows the grapes to ripen gradually. These conditions result in complexities in northern Oregon wines that allow them to compete with world-class wineries.

"You have to really nurture the grapes of a Pinot vine," Anna says quietly. "I'd say we nurture each other. Look at Bob and Dorothy opening their beach house to us this week."

"And not just this week," Ray says. "Several times a summer. Not to mention the way they look out for us when we ride." I have to agree. Bob and Dorothy ride with walkie-talkies fastened to their handlebars and keep each other informed about who is struggling on a hill, needs a rest stop, or missed a turn. No farmer ever tended a vineyard with more care than is lavished on us.

"Let's see," I say with an exaggerated sigh, "That's three—no four strikes and I'm out."

The day is so beautiful, the company so delightful, the wine so smooth, I need to quit talking about my Pinot and just drink it. "To good wine," I say, raising my glass to everyone, "and to even better friends."

Samantha Ducloux Waltz

Wine and Dine with Confidence

Who does not love wine, women,
and song remains a fool
his whole life long.

J. H. Voss

Most people can be divided into two groups: those who appreciate fine wine, and those who don't—and those who don't just can't understand what all the fuss is about.

In my professional life, one of the most important "social" events is the business lunch or dinner. It's where deals can be made or broken, and where first impressions are powerful tools. But it usually begins with one of the most confusing parts of a meal; ordering wine. It's just never as simple as "a scotch and soda, please."

When dining with clients, I always "follow the leader" when it comes to ordering alcohol, but on those occasions where it's appropriate, ordering wine, especially for an entire table, can send anyone who isn't a proud oenophile into insecure, tongue-tied fits—afraid to order any selection for fear of choosing something dreadful, and exposing themselves as a fraud. Wine lovers rejoice, I have a secret that allows everyone at the table, even those who pride themselves on their sensitive palates, to feel they had a part in the selection. It works for anyone who finds themselves in the position of having to order wine for a group without the slightest idea of where to begin. And, I also relish this subtle method as a discreet way to control the spending.

"How about a bottle of wine?" I ask my guests, following up with, "Red . . . or white?" If the response is "White,"

⸙ Taxing Content

The alcohol content in wine determines its taxation rate. U.S. table wine, which is classified as between 7–14 percent alcohol, is taxed at one rate, while wine with a higher concentration of alcohol is taxed at a higher rate.

I respond with, "How about a nice Chardonnay?" Most white wine drinkers enjoy a Chardonnay. If there is any dissention, then I suggest an alternative, such as Pinot Grigio. If the majority chimes in with "Red," I offer, "How about a nice Merlot?" So far, so good. Now here comes the trickery.

Now that I've narrowed down the type of wine, I select two options from the wine list. When our server stops by, I ask which of *those two* she would recommend. A server will likely feel more strongly about one over the other, or will share their opinion of each. You may hear, "This one is light and fruity, while this other one is heavier, more oaky." This is when I turn to my guests and ask for their opinions. "What do you think? Light and crisp? Or the heavier one?"

Once the table has decided which wine they prefer, I turn to our waiter and order confidently. My guests are quite impressed by this time, sure that I have done this a thousand times. Could anything be simpler? And if the server stops by later to ask if we'd like another bottle for the table, I know that it will not be a $400 bottle of Opus One!

Nothing builds relationships better than sharing a meal, and a glass of wine helps to break down barriers. Enjoying a great wine gives us more common ground, more to share, and as we linger over a perfect glass of wine and bond, it feels more like being on holiday than at a business meal.

Robin Jay

Wine and Women

We cannot really love anybody
with whom we never laugh.

Agnes Repplier

The first week of April in 1987 was filled with firsts for me. I had recently celebrated my first year of marriage, I had just flown for the first time, and I was traveling above the Mason-Dixon Line for the first time in order to visit my sister, who was living in Connecticut. As my mother and I arrived at my sister's darling apartment just outside of Hartford, I was ready to commemorate all of these highlights. My sister pulled out a bottle of wine just for the occasion.

The one first that I had not experienced up until that moment, however, was opening a bottle of wine. I had only recently reached the legal drinking age, and besides, my newlywed budget did not include wine with a cork. My mother and sister were also not wine aficionadas. My mother had never opened a bottle of wine in her life, and my sister, an attractive single woman, usually had her wine poured for her at a local night spot.

Despite our lack of expertise, we were three intelligent women, and we were determined to properly celebrate the first night of our visit. After rummaging through her kitchen drawers, my sister was able to locate what appeared to be an ancient corkscrew. I good-naturedly volunteered to do the honors, and attempted to poke the instrument into the cork. It was not as easy as I anticipated. With my mother and sister looking on with great expectations, I grinned and applied a bit more pressure. I finally felt the slightest give and began turning the corkscrew in earnest. I turned and turned.

"Do you need any help?" my sister asked.

"Oh no! I've got it!" I exclaimed as beads of sweat began to form over my eyebrows.

After another couple of uneventful moments and an uncomfortable silence, my sister gently pried the bottle and corkscrew from my clenched fists.

"Come on and let me try. You take a rest," she said.

I reluctantly gave up the bottle and stood back as my sister began her attempt. Throwing her weight into it, she leaned over the bottle and applied immense pressure. I could see her muscles rippling. I could not, however, see the cork budging.

As my sister tried in vain to conquer the cork, I heard my mother, always the resourceful one, plundering through my sister's utensil container. "This is what we need," she exclaimed, brandishing a sharp knife. "Give me that bottle!"

My sister and I both knew better than to argue with our mother, especially when she was armed, so my sister handed over the wine. We watched as Mom used the tip of the knife to carve an indention in the stubborn cork.

When she was satisfied that the opening was the proper depth, she exchanged the knife for the corkscrew and once again attempted to remove the cork. Finally, it appeared that we were getting somewhere, but not fast enough to suit me!

"Let me try again," I said. "I think if I get enough leverage, I can pull it out now!"

My mother relinquished the bottle and handed it to me. I sat on the floor and grasped the bottle not only with my hands but also with my feet! I leaned over and with a grunt and groan began turning and turning. At long last, I felt movement from within!

"I think I've got it!" I squealed pulling upward on the corkscrew. Out popped exactly one half of the cork!

"Oh no!" I moaned. "We're never going to get this opened now!"

I was ready to throw in the corkscrew and concede to the alcohol, but my mother and sister were not giving up yet. We wanted our glass of wine. That bottle represented two generations of women coming together to celebrate their independence, and a corkscrew, or the lack thereof, was not going to conquer us!

Once again, my mother grabbed the trusty knife and with a mighty heave, thrust it into the tattered cork. She twisted and turned and then, much to our surprise, we heard a quiet pop as the cork finally released itself from the confines of its glass prison—and dropped into our liquid refreshment. We watched silently as tiny remnants of cork floated around in the bottle.

I gazed at the three empty wine glasses sitting on the

counter and realized that unless we could transform water into wine, there would be no Chardonnay for us that evening. My sister and I sighed in sheer frustration. *So much for our first evening together,* I thought. Momma's voice broke the silence.

"Where do you keep your coffee filters?" she asked in a very decisive voice.

My sister directed her to the proper cabinet, and I almost reverted to my childhood ways of pouting. I did not want coffee. I wanted a nice, relaxing glass of wine. That is when I took notice of my mother's actions. She carefully placed a coffee filter not in the coffee maker but over a glass and slowly began straining the wine into the goblet. I watched with sheer glee as the liquid streamed into the glass blissfully free of cork! My mother always did have an uncanny ability to improvise in a time of need!

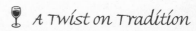

A Twist on Tradition

A comparative blind tasting by experts at the Society of Wine Educator's Conference in 2006 revealed a slight preference for screwcap over natural cork. With the taste uncompromised, proponents of new packaging options are banking on the convenience factor as a strong selling point with consumers.

We drank the entire bottle of wine that evening, and never has a wine tasted so exquisite! The next day, however, we visited a department store and purchased a reliable corkscrew, a welcome addition to my sister's kitchen utensils. These days, I never travel without a corkscrew, but, if I am ever tested again, rest assured that nothing will come between a fine wine and a determined woman!

Terri Duncan

A Final Drive

*The soft extractive note of an
aged cork being withdrawn is the true
sound of a man opening his heart.*

William Samuel Benwell

Years ago, my father developed a casual friendship with the owner of a gas station a mile and a half from his apartment. The fellow's name was Pauli and it was only by chance that Daddy became loyal to his particular set of pumps. Once, driving through that neighborhood, and imagining his front left tire needed air, he pulled into Pauli's place instead of the gas station nearer home where he'd been getting his car serviced for years.

On that occasion, in one of those little twists of fate that changes people's lives, it began to drizzle, When my father turned on his windshield wipers, one broke and began smearing the windshield instead of clearing it of rain. Pauli fiddled with the wiper without being able to fix it, and it was determined that it would have to be replaced. This meant having to order one from the manufacturer, and also meant that Daddy and Pauli would meet again—and as it turned out, again and again, since weeks passed before the wiper arrived at the station. Daddy stopped by every time a drop fell out of the sky to remind Pauli his windshield was still a streaked mess, and that it was taking much too long to get his new wiper. On one of these occasions, Daddy overheard Pauli in a telephone conversation.

"Were you speaking German?" he asked when Pauli emerged from his office.

"I was," Pauli said. One would actually not have had to ask that question, since Pauli's accent alone sounded as if his mouth was full of sauerkraut.

"I also speak German," my father offered. I believe initially his intention was to create an ethnic bond in the interests of expediting the arrival and installation of his windshield wiper. Oddly, neither one of these two German-speaking-middle-Europeans was from Germany. My father was born in Prague, and Pauli was a native of Vienna. I know now that these cities are linked by a three-hour train ride, and that they are in fact bound together not only by language, but by a whole history of similar tradition and cuisine. Although Czechs traditionally love their beer, it also turned out that both my father and Pauli loved a certain Austrian wine, created for generations by a Viennese family named Prager.

The wine lovers' relationship grew. By that I mean that my father began to patronize Pauli's station exclusively. When my father's beloved nine-year-old, twelve-year-old, then fourteen-year-old Buick needed new tires, brakes, or headlights, Pauli came to the rescue. When the car's horn mysteriously began to beep at every left turn, Pauli found the loose wire—no charge. At Christmas, year after year, my father presented Pauli with a bottle of the beloved

Prager wine. Discounts on gas and service followed.

And then, one day, my father asked me if I could go with him to visit his sister Hannah, in Brno.

"Daddy," I said, "Hannah died twenty years ago."

"Oh yes," he said. "It just slipped my mind."

My father's wife and I decided it was time Daddy give up his driver's license and his Buick. We made an appointment with Pauli, but she stayed at home. "I can't watch him part with his car," she said. "I can't. I'll cry. It's his life."

So I was appointed, and followed my father in my own car, first through the car wash, and then to the gas station. There I met Pauli for the first time.

He was a tall man with a gray moustache and eyebrows that looked as if he'd pasted them on. I thought he looked stereotypically Sicilian and nothing like the Austrian oenophile I'd imagined.

"No problem. I find a buyer. You and I have kept that baby in gut shape. Just leave it with me," he said, patting the old Buick's newly-shined hood.

I watched my father step out of his beloved heap and hand the keys to Pauli. I saw the way his shoulders sagged, the glimmer of moisture in his eyes. I wanted to put my arms around him, but didn't do it. It would only emphasize his loss; I held off.

"Wait," Pauli said, as Daddy began to walk away toward the passenger side of my relatively new Honda.

"I brought for this occasion a certain special bottle of wine. We, for sure, have time for a toast to friendship, no?"

As he poured us each a few inches of Prager's red, I saw my father's shoulders straighten, his eyes brighten.

Daddy would be forgetting this moment, and his Buick, very soon. For now, he raised his plastic tumbler and clicked it against Pauli's.

He looked at me. "A little wine? Why not? I'm not driving today." he said.

Pauli raised his "glass" high. "Prosit, my friend!" he said.

"Prosit," Daddy echoed, "to a good friendship," he added, and he finished every drop.

Marlene Fanta Shyer

"I don't know anything about art but
I know what wines I like."

Glossary

Aging is the process by which wine matures. Aging occurs in barrels or bottles and is required to achieve the unique character and complexity of a particular wine.

Appellation is a system of designating geographical and environmental regions that produce fruit with specific characteristics. These regions are typically regulated by a government agency with the goal to protect the quality and marketing integrity of the wine. For example, Burgundy is a region in France, and within Burgundy designated appellations include Chablis and Beaujolais.

Aroma is the natural fragrance that emanates from the fermented grape.

Blending is the mixing of different types of wines from several grape varieties from different vineyards in different combinations until a desired flavor is achieved. Blending evens out acid levels, producing a smoother wine, and ensures that the overall flavor and aroma is more consistent from year to year.

Body can be real or perceived. Real body refers to a wine that is thicker in density, while perceived body is the feel of the wine in the mouth.

Bouquet is the scent released when a bottle is uncorked. Once the bouquet dissipates, the wine is left with the aroma.

Brix is a measurement (in degrees) of the mass ratio of dissolved sugar to water in a liquid. In winemaking, the degree of Brix affects the sweetness, acidity, and alcohol content of a wine.

Chaptalization is a process that increases the alcohol content of finished wine by adding sugar to the must. A higher alcohol content is desirable to prevent bacteria from forming. This does not add to the sweetness of the wine, which is a result of the grape not of chaptalization. California and Italy do not allow chaptalization.

Clarification is the process of removing particles and cloudiness from the fermenting juice. It involves several other processes; racking, filtering, and fining.

Courtier is a wine broker who helps establish the price paid by a négociant to a small producer.

Decanting is the act of gently pouring wine into a serving container, being careful not to disturb the sediments in the bottle. It allows the wine to "breathe" before it is served.

Dessert wine is sweet and high in alcohol, 17–22 percent. Port, Sherry, Madeira, Malaga, Marsala, Muscatel, and Tokay are dessert wines.

Dinner wine is usually light to medium bodied, dry to semi-dry and low to moderate in alcohol by volume (10–13 percent). It is also referred to as table wine.

Dry refers to a wine low in residual sugar.

Earthy is an odor of damp soil perceived in the mouth. This quality diminishes over time, and wines that possess an earthy quality should not be served until they are neutralized by aging two, possibly more, years.

Enzymes are protein molecules that occur naturally in fruit, and can also be purchased commercially. They play a major role in the ripening process by breaking down the natural pectin (water-soluble carbohydrates) in the grapes.

Fermentation is the process of turning grape juice into wine. Glucose (sugar) is broken down into equal parts of ethanol and carbon dioxide in the presence of yeast. Fermentation of red wine generally takes between 5–7 days where white wine typically ferments for 10–14 days.

Filtering removes suspended particles in the liquid during fermentation. Types of filters include a thick layer of cellulose powder (a sheet filter), a thin film of plastic polymer (a membrane filter) with holes smaller than the particles, or a sterile filter that has micro-pores small enough to remove yeast cells if residual sugar exists in the wine at low levels.

Fining is the process of clarifying cloudy or hazy wine by removing suspended particles. Unlike filters, fining agents are used to remove pectin, peptides, iron, or unstable proteins. They are physical agents which absorb the fine particles in the wine and drag them out of the juice into the bottom of the tank or barrel, where they will be removed by racking. They can also be chemical agents which form a bond with hydrogen elements in the undesirable particles. Fining agents can be casein, bentonite, charcoal, or egg whites. In ancient times, animal blood was used.

Finish is the aftertaste, texture, and mouth-feel that lingers after wine is swallowed.

Flat is a term connoting insufficient acidity. Some acidity is essential in wine or the taste is flat and medicinal.

Flight is a sampling of several wines that allows exploration of different wines without having to commit to an entire glass or bottle.

Hang time the total number of days grapes stay on the vine before harvest.

Legs is a coating on the inside of a wine glass after being swirled that separates into rivulets that slide down the glass. It indicates a rich, full-bodied wine.

Must is the unfermented juice of crushed, newly-harvested grapes.

Négociant is a dealer who sells and ships wine as a wholesaler. They buy grapes and sometimes blended product from smaller growers and winemakers, and then bottle and ship wine under their own labels.

Nose is the smell of a wine, both its aroma and bouquet, which reveals the character of the base from which the wine is made.

Oenophile is a wine connoisseur.

Pairing is the process of matching food and wine with an eye toward synergy and balance in the characteristics of both. The wine shouldn't overpower the food, nor should the food overpower the wine. Just like condiments, wine should compliment the food.

Pips are the seeds found in grapes.

Pomace is the highly-compacted mass of skin, pulp, and pips remaining after pressing. It is an excellent source of nitrogen and often dumped between vineyard rows. In France and Italy the pomace is distilled into grappa (Italy) and marc (France).

Pressing is the process of extracting the grape's juices, colors, and tannins from the skins. Over-pressing can result in an unfavorable taste in the end product. Red wines are pressed after the fermentation process has begun. Whites are pressed as unfermented must.

Racking is the first step of the clarification process where insoluble matter at the bottom of the tanks or barrels is left behind as the liquid on the surface is poured into another container. Racking can lead to over-oxygenation of the wine.

A *Sommelier,* or wine steward, is a trained wine professional who is involved in wine procurement, storage, and rotation. A sommelier develops the wine list at finer restaurants and is responsible for the delivery of wine service and training for other restaurant staff. Working with the chef, the Sommelier pays special attention to the pairing of wine and food, and duties can encompass beers, whiskies, cigars, even water.

Sulphating is the process of sterilization, preferable to pasteurization, used in winemaking to kill off wild yeast and other unwanted microorganisms. It also prevents oxidation of the must.

Table wine is a low-alcohol content wine suitable for being served with a meal. In Europe, table wine typically is not permitted to disclose its region of production, and represents the lowest quality level of wine produced.

Tannins are naturally occurring compounds in vegetables and flowers. In grapes they are found in the skins and pips, which are extracted during the winemaking process. Some are harsh and bitter, others are round and pleasing. Some taste unripe, others mature. Tannins are what give red wine that puckery, astringent sensation that leaves your mouth feeling dry, and they are critical in the development of a red wine's flavor and texture.

Tasting notes are records kept by vinters during vinification to describe the qualities and nuances of wine.

Terroir is a term that commonly refers to the variables in a grapevine's environment that contribute to a wine's flavor, texture, and aroma.

Texture is the impression on the palate left by dense, full-bodied wines.

Thin is a wine lacking in body, with the viscosity of water.

Varietal is a wine made from a single variety of grape or named after the principal grape in its composition.

Vinification is the act of winemaking.

Vintner is a winemaker.

Viticulturalist is the grape grower.

More Chicken Soup?

We would love to hear your reactions to the stories in this book. Please let us know what your favorite stories were and how they affected you.

Many of the stories and poems you have read in this book were submitted by readers like you who had read earlier Chicken Soup for the Soul books. We publish several Chicken Soup for the Soul books every year. We invite you to contribute a story to one of these future volumes.

Stories may be up to 1,200 words and must uplift or inspire. You may submit an original piece, something you have read, or your favorite quotation on your refrigerator door.

To obtain a copy of our submission guidelines and a listing of upcoming Chicken Soup books, please write, fax or check our websites. Please send your submissions to:

Chicken Soup for the Soul
P.O. Box 30880 Santa Barbara, CA 93130
fax: 805-563-2945
website: www.chickensoup.com

Just send a copy of your stories and other pieces to the above address. We will be sure that both you and the author are credited for your submission.

For information about speaking engagements, other books, audiotapes, workshops and training programs, please contact any of our authors directly.

Supporting Others

All over the world, millions of innocent people are caught up in intolerable situations. But they are not today's victims; they are tomorrow's heroes, who have the power to transform their own communities.

The publisher and authors of *Chicken Soup for the Chocolate Lover's Soul, Tea Lover's Soul, Coffee Lover's Soul,* and *Wine Lover's Soul* are pleased to donate five cents from the sale of each of these four books, up to a maximum of $1 million per book, to Mercy Corps, an organization that exists to alleviate suffering, poverty and oppression by helping people build secure, productive and just communities.

Mercy Corps works amid disasters, conflicts, chronic poverty, and instability to unleash the potential of people who can win against nearly impossible odds. Since 1979, Mercy Corps has provided $1.3 billion in assistance to people in 100 nations. Supported by headquarters offices in North America, Europe, and Asia, the agency's unified global programs employ 3,400 staff worldwide and reach nearly 14.4 million people in more than thirty-five countries.

Mercy Corps has learned that communities recovering from war or social upheaval must be the agents of their own transformation for change to endure. It's only when communities set their own agendas, raise their own resources, and implement programs themselves, that their first successes result in the renewed hope, confidence and skills to continue development.

Your purchase of this title has helped support Mercy Corps, but if you would like to do more or would like more information about the great work they do, please contact them.

Mercy Corps
3015 SW 1st Avenue
Portland, OR 97201
phone: (800) 292-3355
website: www.mercycorps.org

Who Is Jack Canfield?

Jack Canfield is the cocreator and editor of the Chicken Soup for the Soul series, which Time magazine has called "the publishing phenomenon of the decade." The series now has 105 titles with over 100 million copies in print in forty-one languages. Jack is also the coauthor of eight other bestselling books, including *The Success Principles: How to Get from Where You Are to Where You Want to Be, Dare to Win, The Aladdin Factor, You've Got to Read This Book,* and *The Power of Focus: How to Hit Your Business, Personal and Financial Targets with Absolute Certainty.*

Jack has recently developed a telephone coaching program and an online coaching program based on his most recent book, *The Success Principles.* He also offers a seven-day Breakthrough to Success seminar every summer, which attracts 400 people from fifteen countries around the world.

Jack is the CEO of Chicken Soup for the Soul Enterprises and the Canfield Training Group in Santa Barbara, California, and founder of the Foundation for Self-Esteem in Culver City, California. He has conducted intensive personal and professional development seminars on the principles of success for over 900,000 people in twenty-one countries around the world. He has spoken to hundreds of thousands of others at numerous conferences and conventions, and has been seen by millions of viewers on national television shows such as *The Today Show, Fox and Friends, Inside Edition, Hard Copy, CNN's Talk Back Live, 20/20, Eye to Eye,* the *NBC Nightly News,* and the *CBS Evening News.*

Jack is the recipient of many awards and honors, including three honorary doctorates and a Guinness World Records Certificate for having seven Chicken Soup for the Soul books appearing on the *New York Times* bestseller list on May 24, 1998.

To write to Jack or for inquiries about Jack as a speaker, his coaching programs or his seminars, use the following contact information:

The Canfield Companies
P.O. Box 30880 • Santa Barbara, CA 93130
phone: 805-563-2935 • fax: 805-563-2945
e-mail: info@jackcanfield.com • website: www.jackcanfield.com

Who Is Mark Victor Hansen?

In the area of human potential, no one is more respected than Mark Victor Hansen. For more than thirty years, Mark has focused solely on helping people from all walks of life reshape their personal vision of what's possible. His powerful messages of possibility, opportunity and action have created powerful change in thousands of organizations and millions of individuals worldwide.

He is a sought-after keynote speaker, bestselling author, and marketing maven. Mark's credentials include a lifetime of entrepreneurial success and an extensive academic background. He is a prolific writer with many bestselling books, such as *The One Minute Millionaire, The Power of Focus, The Aladdin Factor,* and *Dare to Win,* in addition to the Chicken Soup for the Soul series. Mark has made a profound influence through his library of audios, videos, and articles in the areas of big thinking, sales achievement, wealth building, publishing success, and personal and professional development.

Mark is the founder of the MEGA Seminar Series. MEGA Book Marketing University and Building Your MEGA Speaking Empire are annual conferences where Mark coaches and teaches new and aspiring authors, speakers, and experts on building lucrative publishing and speaking careers. Other MEGA events include MEGA Marketing Magic and My MEGA Life. He has appeared on television (*Oprah, CNN,* and *The Today Show*), in print (*Time, U.S. News & World Report, USA Today, New York Times,* and *Entrepreneur*) and on countless radio interviews, assuring our planet's people that "you can easily create the life you deserve."

As a philanthropist and humanitarian, Mark works tirelessly for organizations such as Habitat for Humanity, American Red Cross, March of Dimes, Childhelp USA, and many others. He is the recipient of numerous awards that honor his entrepreneurial spirit, philanthropic heart, and business acumen. He is a lifetime member of the Horatio Alger Association of Distinguished Americans, an organization that honored Mark with the prestigious Horatio Alger Award for his extraordinary life achievements. Mark Victor Hansen is an enthusiastic crusader of what's possible and is driven to make the world a better place.

Mark Victor Hansen & Associates, Inc.
P.O. Box 7665 • Newport Beach, CA 92658
phone: 949-764-2640 • fax: 949-722-6912
website: www.markvictorhansen.com

Who Is Theresa Peluso?

Theresa has always felt drawn to a page and the power of words. Books represent knowledge, expression, freedom, adventure, creativity, and escape—so it's no surprise that her life has revolved around books.

Her career began over thirty years ago in a large publisher's book-club operation. In 1981, Theresa joined Health Communications, a fledgling publisher that grew to become the country's #1 self-help publisher, home to groundbreaking *New York Times* bestsellers and the series recognized as a publishing phenomenon, Chicken Soup for the Soul.

Theresa is the coauthor of *Chicken Soup for the Horse Lover's Soul, Chicken Soup for the Horse Lover's Soul II, Chicken Soup for the Recovering Soul, Chicken Soup for the Recovering Soul Daily Inspirations, Chicken Soup for the Shopper's Soul, Chicken Soup for the Dieter's Soul,* and *Chicken Soup for the Coffee Lover's Soul.*

She lives in south Florida with her husband, Brian, who shares her appreciation for a good Chianti to celebrate their Italian roots, and their two felines, one of whom has developed a fetish for corks. Contact Theresa at:

Health Communications, Inc.
3201 SW 15th Street • Deerfield Beach, FL 33442
phone: 954-360-0909 • fax: 954-418-0844
e-mail: teri@wineloverssoul.com • website: www.hcibooks.com

contributors

The stories in this book are original pieces or taken from previously published sources, such as books, magazines, and newspapers. If you would like to contact any of the contributors for information about their writing or would like to invite them to speak in your community, look for their contact information included in their biography.

Kathleen A. Alcorn is a native of Springfield, Illinois. She is a graduate of Lincoln Land Community College, Southern Illinois University at Carbondale, and holds an M.F.A. from Savannah College of Art and Design.

Diana M. Amadeo received the 2006 Catholic Press Association Book Award for *Holy Friends: Thirty Saints and Blesseds of the Americas*. (Pauline Books and Media). She also sports a bit of pride in having 450 publications with her byline. Yet, she humbly, persistently, tweaks and rewrites her thousand or so rejections with eternal hope that they may yet see the light of day. Diana lives in her woodsy writer's hideaway in New England with her husband of thirty-one years. Two daughters, a son and daughter-in-law live ever so close in her heart.

Aaron Bacall's work has appeared in most national publications and several cartoon collections, and has been used for advertising, greeting cards, wall calendars, and several corporate promotional books. Three of his cartoons are featured in the permanent collection at the Harvard Business School's Baker Library. Aaron can be reached at abacall@msn.com.

Carolyn Boni is the mother of two and stepmother of eight, five of whom are in college or married and have made a granddad out of Carolyn's husband five times. Carolyn, who is also a registered nurse, lives on a 102-acre farm, complete with cows, horses, chickens, rabbits, eieioooo.

Rod G. Boriack grew up surrounded by vineyards in Lodi, California and now lives in Chicago, Illinois, editing, writing, and doing other stuff for the Evangelical Lutheran Church in America. Rod's wife, two twenty-something kids, a grandson, motorcycle, and about a dozen bottles of wine form his family unit.

Eric S. Brent is a teacher in New York City and a freelance wine consultant with over twenty-five years in the New York wine trade. He has worked for Zachy's of Scarsdale, managed Rochambeau of Westchester, and currently works as a consultant for Katonah Wines.

Minnie Norton Browne lives in historic Granbury, Texas. She is a wife, mother of two children, grandmother of four grandchildren, an artist, a retired school teacher, a Court Appointed Child Advocate, and active in her church. Minnie has written articles for the magazine *Granbury Showcase*, been published in *Langdon Review of the Arts* in Texas, and has had poems and a memoir story published in *Chips off the Writers' Bloc*.

Isabel Bearman Bucher's work ranges from research to stories of the heart. With Robert, her husband of twenty-eight years, she travels the world on home exchanges; enjoys four children, five grandchildren, and one great-grandson. Her book, *Nonno's Monkey, An Italian American Memoir* is set in the 1940's, and told from an oft-confused, six-year-old point of view. Visit Isabel at www.oneitaliana.com.

Kathe Campbell lives on a western Montana mountain with her national champion mammoth donkeys, her precious Keeshond, and a few kitties. Three grown children, eleven grands and three greats round out the herd. She has contributed to newspapers and national magazines on Alzheimer's disease, and her Montana stories are found on many e-zines. Kathe is a contributing author to the Chicken Soup for the Soul series, *People Who Make A Difference*, various anthologies, *RX for Writers*, magazines, and medical journals.

Pamela Christian is passionate about life. Sharing her Christian faith and embracing God's blessings, even in adversity, describes her daily life. She's a woman of many talents: a gourmet cook, lavish home entertainer, television and radio host, retreat and conference speaker, writer, author, Bible study teacher, wife, and mother. She and her family reside in Yorba Linda, California. Visit Pam at www.pamelachristianministries.com.

Elsa Kok Colopy is a passionate author and speaker. She's written four books and hundreds of articles. She also travels around the country, leading retreats and conferences for a variety of audiences. Elsa is based out of Bella Vista, Arkansas. Together, she and her husband, Brian, have four children. Her website is www.elsakokcolopy.com.

Ron Coleman began cartooning as a teenager. He read an ad in *Popular Mechanics* magazine which said, "Earn Big Money Drawing Simple Cartoons." He hasn't ever earned any big money, and he has found cartoons are not all that simple to draw, but he's been at it for about forty years. Visit Ron at www.coleman-cartoons.com.

Cookie Curci is a freelance writer whose work has been published in books, national newspapers, magazines, and on websites, and has appeared in a weekly column in her community newspaper for fifteen years. Cookie credits her Italian-American family as the source of her inspiration for her work. This is the ninth story she has contributed to the Chicken Soup for the Soul series.

Valeria X. D'Alcantara is a horsewoman by dawn, a computer geek by day and a writer by night with a YA novel currently under consideration. She enjoys cooking for her wonderful family and tending to her horses, dogs, cats, and chickens. Born in Washington, D.C., she now calls North Carolina home.

Star Davies resides in Wisconsin with her husband and stepson. In addition to writing, she is an Event Coordinator of Legend Images Photography. The birth of her godsons inspired Star to create the eleven-book fantasy series in which her stories now live.

Terri Duncan received her bachelor's, master's, and specialist's degrees in education from Augusta State University. She is currently a Graduation Coach in Evans, Georgia and is also a devoted wife and the mother of two delightful teenagers. Her dream is to have published a full-length book suitable for children.

Greg Faherty is well-published in the areas of fiction, nonfiction, and poetry, including several stories in the Chicken Soup for the Soul series. He is also the owner and operator of www.a-perfect-resume.com, an internet resume service. He and his wife enjoy exercising with their dogs, cooking healthy meals, and relaxing with a glass of good wine.

Catherine Fallis is the fifth woman in the world to have earned the title of Master Sommelier. She created www.planetgrape.com and *the grape goddess® guides to good living*, is an instructor at the Culinary Institute of America and Professional Culinary Institute, and opens Champagne with a sword in a dazzling three-minute theatrical performance.

Louise Foerster has savored wine the world over with friends and family. The pleasure of an extraordinary glass of wine infuses her with the will to write, walk, read, and enjoy life in a civilized way.

Jonny Hawkins has been cartooning professionally since 1986. His work has appeared in over 370 publications, such as *Reader's Digest, Forbes, Boy's Life,* and *Woman's World.* His books, including *The Awesome Book of Healthy Humor,* and his *Cartoon-A-Day* calendars are available everywhere.

Lori Hein is the author of *Ribbons of Highway: A Mother-Child Journey Across America* and a contributor to several Chicken Soup for the Soul book titles. Her writing and photography have appeared in publications nationwide and online. She publishes a world travel blog at RibbonsofHighway.blogspot.com, and you can visit her at www.LoriHein.com.

Abha Iyengar is a writer, poet, cyber-artist, activist, yoga enthusiast, and photographer. She loves to travel and experience the new. Her work has appeared in *Chicken Soup for the Soul, Healthy Living* series, *Knit Lit Too, The Simple Touch of Fate, Arabesques Review, Scribe Spirit, Kritya, riverbabble,* and *flashquake,* among others. Connect with Abha at abhaiyengar@gmail.com.

Nancy Jackson lives with her husband and son in Oregon. Her true stories have also been published in *Sacred Waters, Haunted Encounters: Departed Family and Friends,* and *Romancing the Soul.* She has also published romance under the name Ann Cory.

Robin Jay is the award-winning author of *The Art of the Business Lunch—Building Relationships Between 12 and 2,* a professional speaker, corporate trainer, and president of the Las Vegas Convention Speakers Bureau.

Ruth Jones worked in organizational development for over twenty-five years. A year ago she gave up her consulting practice and started writing. She has completed the first draft of her first novel and has plans for a second one. Ruth lives in Tennessee with her husband, Terry.

Dawn Josephson is a writing coach to nonfiction authors. She has ghostwritten and/or personally authored 2,500 published articles and twenty published books. She is the author of *Putting It On Paper*, coauthor of *Write It Right*, and creator of the Better Writing Now Toolkit. Visit Dawn at www.betterwritingnow.com.

Joyce Uhernik Kurzawski resides in Pittsburgh, Pennsylvania. Retired, she is married with one adult son and cares for an elderly parent while she maintains two households (her family's home and her mother's). The proud owner of two cats, she's involved with animal rehabilitation efforts.

Kelley J. P. Lindberg has written dozens of how-to books, essays, and feature articles. She has also raced hermit crabs in the British Virgin Islands, sipped coffee with a scarf vendor in Jerusalem, slept in an Irish nunnery, kept a rendezvous in Venice, snorkeled with a shark in Belize, and—more important—learned to order wine in half-a-dozen languages.

Patricia Lorenz is the coauthor of three Chicken Soup for the Soul books, has stories in over thirty other editions, and is the author of: *Life's Too Short to Fold Your Underwear*, *Grab the Extinguisher My Birthday Cake's On Fire*, *Great American Outhouse Stories*, *True Pilot Stories*, *A Hug A Day for Single Parents*, and *Stuff That Matters for Single Parents*. She is an award-winning journalist, has been featured in seventeen *Daily Guideposts* books and over sixty anthologies, has over 400 articles and shorts to her credit, and is a sought-after speaker for women's retreats and writing conferences.

Loree Lough is a best-selling author whose stories have earned numerous awards. Loree teaches writing and frequently shares industry insights with audiences in the U.S. and abroad. She and her husband live in Maryland with a formerly abused, now-spoiled Pointer. For more information visit www.loreelough.com.

Karen M. Lynch is a freelance writer and journalist. She enjoys her Pinot in Connecticut where she lives with her husband and their three children. This is her second contribution to a Chicken Soup anthology; her essay "Momma's Girl" appeared in *Chicken Soup for the Shopper's Soul*. E-mail Karen at karenmlynch@gmail.com or visit her web site at www.karenmlynch.com.

Laura Marble is a staff writer for the *Explorer* newspaper in Tucson where she writes "Field Trips," a weekly column that offers glimpses into often unexplored territories and reminds readers they can find opportunities for meaningful experiences just about anywhere. She has a master's degree in journalism from the University of Missouri. Contact her at lemarble@juno.com.

Gail Gaymer Martin is a multiple award-winning author who writes for Steeple Hill and Barbour Publishing. Gail has signed forty fiction contracts and has over

1 million books in print. Gail is a keynote speaker and teaches writing at conferences across the U.S. She has a master's degree from Wayne State University in Michigan.

Gay N. Martin is a member of the Society of American Travel Writers and International Food, Wine, and Travel Writers Association, and the author of *Off the Beaten Path Alabama, Off the Beaten Path Louisiana* (The Globe Pequot Press), and *Alabama's Historic Restaurants and Their Recipes* (John F. Blair, Publisher). Visit Gay at www.gn martintravels.com.

Alf B. Meier is a photographer whose work has taken him around the globe. His credits include *International Living, I Love Cats, Athens News* and *The International Railway Traveler*. His Website is http://www.travelwriters.com/Alf.

Milan Moyer (pen name) is the author of several books. Her articles about health and wellness have been featured in local and national newspapers and magazines. She is an award-winning producer of public affairs radio and television shows.

Cari Noga is a freelance writer who lives in Michigan with her husband and son. She writes a blog on the regional wine industry. Visit Cari at www.michgrapevine. com.

Diane C. Perrone holds a M.A. in Advertising/Education and is mother of seven. She is a Christian woman, spouse, teacher, public speaker to "seasoned citizens," and those who market to them, Mary Kay Cosmetics consultant, and "Grandma Di" to fifteen. She writes from Franklin, Wisconsin, "between babies."

Stephanie Piro is one of King Feature's team of women cartoonists and is the Saturday chick in "Six Chix." Stephanie's line of gift items, available from her company, Strip T's, can be seen on www.stephaniepiro.com, and her new book, *My Cat Loves Me Naked,* is available at bookstores everywhere. Contact Stephanie by e-mailing stephaniepiro@verizon.net, or writing 27 River Road, Farmington, NH 03835.

Carol McAdoo Rehme directs a nonprofit agency, Vintage Voices Inc. She is a prolific writer, editor, and coauthor of numerous gift books. Her latest project, *Chicken Soup for the Empty Nester's Soul,* will be released in 2008. Self-pampering helps maintain her sanity—and vanilla bean tea is just the ticket! Contact her at carol@rehme.com.

Maureen Rigney is a Licensed Clinical Social Worker who grew up in South Dakota and now works for the Lung Cancer Alliance in Washington, D.C. area. She is an avid traveler and, usually with her friend Barbara Pollack, has visited fourteen countries in the past thirteen years. She has also been known to enjoy a good bottle of wine, although finding her favorite Moroccan vintage has proven to be a challenge.

Harry Rubin retired from the Army in 1975 and began a second career writing a column in the Sunday edition of a newspaper. His short stories have been published in magazines. Harry writes poetry and has published *Limericks and Other Stuff.* He has completed a memoir, a biography, and two novels, *Chasing Pirates* and *The Counterfeit War.* Find out more at his website: http://BardOfHinesville.com.

Colette J. Sasina and her husband, John, were married in 1961 and are the parents of five children and the grandparents of nine. Colette enjoys the luminosity and camaraderie of the Del Webb Spruce Creek Country Club Writers' Bloc in Summerfield, Florida. Occasionally, her poems are published locally.

Marlene Shyer has written eleven books for children, two plays, five novels, and a memoir, coauthored with her son, Christopher Shyer. In addition, she is the author over one hundred short stories and articles published in women's magazines, and most recently has written about travel for newspapers and magazines.

Stuart Jay Silverman is a food writer for *The Chicago Tribune, Chicago Reader, Gault-Millau,* and other affiliated Tribune outlets. Stuart coauthored *The Ozarks Traveler* with his wife, Sondra Rosenberg, is the author of *The Complete Lost Poems* (Hawk Publishing Group), nearly 400 poems, and has been published in some 100 anthologies and magazines. Born in Brooklyn, he taught college for twenty-seven years in Alabama and Illinois. Retired, he divides his time between Chicago and Hot Springs, Arkansas.

Jean Stewart is a writer in Mission Viejo, California, mother of twin daughters, and is still sharing the joys of good wine with her husband of forty-six years. Her family, parenting, and travel stories can be found in other Chicken Soup for the Soul books, as well as in newspapers and magazines.

Elva Stoelers' work has been published in Chicken Soup for the Soul books, other anthologies, a variety of parenting magazines in Canada and Australia, and broadcast on CBC Radio Canada. She would like to extend a heart felt thank you to Nellie and Lloyd, vintners extrodinaire, for fun and fond memories. Cheers!

Samantha Ducloux Waltz is an award-winning freelance writer in Portland, Oregon. Her essays can be found in a number of current anthologies and in the *Christian Science Monitor.* She has also published adult nonfiction and juvenile fiction under the names Samantha Ducloux and Samellyn Wood.

Bobbe White is a Certified Laughter Leader (Seriously!). Bobbe is a banker by day and speaker on workplace humor/laughter therapy when the scheduling gods permit it. She is the author of *Life in the Laugh Lane,* and coauthor of *Fantastic Customer Service.* Bobbe is a member of the National Speakers Association, the Association for Applied/Therapeutic Humor, the National Association Female Executives, the World Laughter Tour, and President of Try Laughter! Inc.

David R. Wilkins is the VP of Manufacturing Operations at Aragon Surgical by day, and the author of several Chicken Soup for the Soul stories by night (*Father's Soul, Bride's Soul, Recovering Soul* and *Recovering Soul Daily Inspirations*). David is currently shopping his novel for representation and lives with his wife in San Jose, California.

Cheryl Elaine Williams is a freelance writer residing in western Pennsylvania. She enjoys family activities, attending writers' conferences, gardening, and raising pet parakeets.

Permissions *(continued from page iv)*

Opposites Attract. Reprinted by permission of Catherine Fallis. ©1999 Catherine Fallis. Originally appeared in *grape goddess® guides to good living, WINE* by Catherine Fallis.

The Makings of a Sommelier. Reprinted by permission of Pamela Christian. ©2006 Pamela Christian.

From Jug to Cork. Reprinted by permission of David R. Wilkins. ©2007 David R. Wilkins.

A Box of Wine. Reprinted by permission of Tammy Davies. ©2007 Tammy Davies.

Share This Wine With Me! Reprinted by permission of Joyce Stark. ©2005 Joyce Stark.

To Wine . . . or Not to Wine. Reprinted by permission of Bobbe White. ©2007 Bobbe White.

The Greatest Vintage. Reprinted by permission of Karen M. Lynch. ©2007 Karen M. Lynch.

Champagne and Fortune Cookies. Reprinted by permission of Gaymer Martin. ©2007 Gaymer Martin.

The Secret Ingredient. Reprinted by permission of Kathleen A. Alcorn. ©2006 Kathleen A. Alcorn.

Apricots and Vermentino. Reprinted by permission of Lori Hein. ©2007 Lori Hein.

Chanson du Vin (was titled *Wine* song). Reprinted by permission of Louise Foerster. ©2007 Louise Foerster.

A Taste of New Wine. Reprinted by permission of Minnie Norton Browne. ©2007 Minnie Norton Browne.

Nonno's Wine. Reprinted by permission of Isabel Bearman Bucher. ©2006 Isabel Bearman Bucher.

The Soup. Reprinted by permission of Diane Perrone. ©2007 Diane Perrone.

How (Not) to Open a Bottle of Champagne. Reprinted by permission of Ruth Jones. ©2007 Ruth Jones.

Doña Felica's Vineyard. Reprinted by permission of Alf B. Meier. ©2007 Alf B. Meier.

Blame it on the Wine. Reprinted by permission of Patricia Lorenz. ©2007 Patricia Lorenz.

A Glass of Bliss. Reprinted by permission of Greg Faherty. ©2007 Greg Faherty.

Muscat Cannelli. Reprinted by permission of Valeria X. D'Alcantara. ©2007 Valeria X. D'Alcantara.

Passing the Cork. Reprinted by permission of Colette J. Sasina. ©2006 Colette J. Sasina.

An Ounce of Prevention (was: *Papa's Red Wine*). Reprinted by permission of Cookie Curci. ©1987 Cookie Curci. Previously published in *Las Vegas LaVoce,* June 2004.

The Start of a Beautiful Friendship. Reprinted by permission of Maureen Rigney. ©2007 Maureen Rigney.